# PHENOMENOLOGY
# AND
# RELIGION

*HERMENEUTICS: VOLUME V*

# HERMENEUTICS
## Studies in the History of Religions

# Phenomenology and Religion

*Structures of the*
*Christian Institution*

*HENRY DUMÉRY*

UNIVERSITY OF CALIFORNIA PRESS

BERKELEY, LOS ANGELES, LONDON

University of California Press
Berkeley and Los Angeles, California

University of California Press, Ltd.
London, England

ISBN: 0-520-02714-0
Library of Congress Catalog Card Number: 73-94443
Printed in the United States of America

Originally published as
*Phénoménologie et religion:
Structures de l'institution chrétienne*
© 1958, Presses Universitaires de France
English translation © copyright 1975 by The Regents of
the University of California

# Translator's Preface

Like so many other things in this technological world of ours, this translation is the work of many minds.

The idea of doing the translation occurred to me while I was conducting a lengthy correspondence with Professor Duméry on his work in the philosophy of religion, and when I suggested the project to him, he readily gave his assent. As the work of translation progressed, I kept in constant touch with Professor Duméry and, I'm afraid, quite pestered him with a veritable stream of questions about the precise meaning or interpretation of words, phrases, and even whole passages. Fortunately for me, he was very cooperative and patiently answered all my queries.

During this time I was stationed at our house of philosophy, St. Bonaventure's, Cork, Ireland, and some of my confrères there were on the faculty of University College, Cork, one of the three campuses of the National University of Ireland. These confrères were: Rev. Brendan E. O'Mahoney, Professor of Philosophy; Rev. Cuthbert McCann, Assistant Lecturer in Philosophy; and Rev. Peter R. Demsey, Professor of Applied Psychology —all of whom were most generous in helping me with the translation.

When the manuscript was finished, I sent it to Robert Y. Zachary, the Los Angeles Editor of the University of California Press. Mr. Zachary accepted it for publication and then went to work on it in his own inimitably skillful way, pulling it together, smoothing out the rough patches and clarifying the obscurities. It is to Mr. Zachary principally that the book owes its final form.

August 22, 1974          Paul Barrett, O.F.M.Cap.

# Preface

My aim in this book is to trace in broad outline the phenomenology of the Christian experience, or rather, of the Christian *institution*.

The object of these pages is not to prove anything but to understand and to bring understanding. When an institution is in question, to understand means to recover from its structures the origin and establishment of meaning. I shall try to clarify that meaning, to describe those structures. I shall do it rationally and freely, as a philosopher. More precisely, I shall do it as a phenomenologist, taking care to go to the things themselves (die Sachen selbst), and doing my utmost not to falsify or force anything.

Only in one place have I departed from this aim, and that is in chapter 4, where the reader will find some bits and pieces of an overall judgment.

I shall reach no conclusions. Not, however, because the subject does not warrant conclusions, but because I wish to leave it to the reader to arrive at them.

H. D.

# Contents

# 1. Christianity and Institution

Christianity is an *established* religion, an *instituted* religion—and these words have several meanings. They mean, first, that Christianity is not an empty religious *form*, a form without content; next, that it is not a shapeless religious *experience,* an experience devoid of structure; and finally, that it is not an essentially subjective view of God, lacking intersubjective expressions, especially those associated with divine worship.

## Positive or Manifest Religion

As against formalism, Christianity is a positive religion; as against pragmatism, Christian practice is based on doctrine; and as against subjectivism, Christian piety is taught and exercised in community, for Christian prayer and contemplation, although they sometimes seem to be solitary exercises, are in fact closely linked— on the one hand to official dogmatic teaching, that is, to the creed of the Church, and on the other hand to community devotion, the praying and worshipping together of ritual.

Thus Christianity is neither a "moral faith" in the sense in which Kant sets *moral faith* over against *statutory faith,* nor an instinctive feeling, like the simple peasant faith of the Savoyard Vicar; nor is it even a mysticism which the individual cultivates aside from the group. These three interpretations are immediately eliminated when one accepts, with Hegel, that Christianity is a *manifest* religion, that it exists only in its manifestations, and that these manifestations are concerned at once with personal life and community life.

It is clear, then, why Christianity resists every philosophy except a philosophy of institution.

## The Problem of the Institutional Bond

To arrive at the meaning of Christianity it is not sufficient to indulge in an analysis of concepts, because the Christian categories are not bound together in a purely ideal order, nor do they form a system, a bundle of abstractions, as it were. Rather they define a style of life and are a guide to practical living.

Nor is it sufficient merely to list a series of crucial events, because the events upon which Christianity is founded are never left in their raw state, that is to say, they are never confined to the merely secular sphere but are rather "indoctrinated" events, events which are selected, interpreted, and "validated" by faith.

It is not even sufficient to remark that there is a bond between history and dogma, thereby bringing together into one perspective what the believer learns and what he believes, because the whole problem is to find out, not whether there is a connection between history and dogma, but what that connection is; not whether there is a principle of unification, but what kind of principle it is.

It goes without saying that such a bond exists and that such a unification can be made out between doctrine and history, because faith cannot exist unless such a condition is fulfilled. But if the how and the why of such a bond are not made clear, the manner of the Christian affirmation will escape us. In fact, it did escape Spinoza, Kant, Brunschvicg, and Alain, who saw on the one side ideal categories and on the other contingent actualities; and the connection between the two seemed to them accidental, precarious, and often arbitrary.

Where these philosophers came to grief, a phenomenology of institution can and must succeed: a phenomenology of *instituted meaning*, of meaning that takes on body from events, of events that acquire form from historical interpretation. It can do so because it arrives at meaning, not by way of categories alone nor by way of facts alone, but integrally and directly, through the intentional relation that man has with the world and with history. And since such a phenomenology can succeed, it must succeed, because all human behavior has meaning; and there is no reason to assume *a priori* that only religious behavior is devoid of meaning. Those who, despite the testimony of believers, risk such an hypothesis give proof that they have become strangers to a whole area of human expression. They forget that without myths and religions, without symbolisms, even the most naive symbolisms, neither science nor philosophy would have been born.

It is therefore the institutional bond of Christianity which is the paramount problem. In truth it is the sole problem, the one from which flow all the others; and hence it becomes evident that only a phenomenology of institution has any chance of solving it.

*The Phenomenological Method*

And what are the questions that will go to form such

a phenomenology; or rather, what themes will it have to develop? It is impossible to answer this question in advance because no phenomenology of institution can be elaborated in the abstract. A phenomenology arises only from reading and studying the phenomena, and welcoming whatever presents itself. A phenomenology of institution is possible only in terms of given institutions and only as a specific meaning appears in the concrete structures. In describing Christianity, the phenomenologist finds one of the cases where he can hope to discover the vital links which are part of the dynamics of every institution. Hence such a description of Christianity is a sample of a phenomenology of institution, a limited but valid sample.

This restriction of our field must not make us forget that many other analyses would be necessary to clarify fully the idea of institution, and that, in order to be quite clear about the method employed, we would have to begin by questioning the method itself. But such a procedure would lead us too far from our subject, and we would, in the end, have to define the boundaries of every phenomenology. Nonetheless, a phenomenology of institution is both possible and profitable, and a phenomenology of the Christian institution especially holds out much promise.

At first glance the Christian institution is disconcerting because it is at once complex and subtle, adaptable enough to absorb the most disparate elements, yet demanding and intractable to the point of seeming rigid, even exclusive. It would be futile to attempt to sum it up in a simple formula or to give a consistent definition of it, if one did not have the chance to compare it with that even more ancient institution from which it sprang, namely, the Jewish institution. Christianity is a Judaism— and it is this we must show. When compared with Judaism, Christianity evinces similarities and differences which are equally suggestive, and which will enable us to place it—to compare it with its model and to specify its nature.

# 2. The Jewish Institution

Like Judaism, Christianity is a *historical* religion, a *typological* religion; it is a *particular* expression of religion, but is *universal* in scope. This triple characteristic is of Jewish origin, even in the eyes of the historians of Israel who regard Christianity as a Greek schism. Thus a knowledge of Judaism is important for a knowledge of Christianity.

We are accordingly going to study these three characteristics in the Jewish institution, so as to understand better the Christian institution. Of course, these attributes interest us here, not as contingent facts, but only insofar as they are "structures." Furthermore, we shall not have to trace in detail their evolution, but only to explore their meaning.

*Historical Revelation*

The principal discovery of the Jewish people was that history is revelatory. For all pagan civilizations it is nature and not history that reveals God and expresses the divine. For the pagans any part of the material world—a stone, a wellspring, a tree, the sun, the moon, the sky, the earth, etc.—can take on a sacred value. To all appearances the symbolism that lies behind these material signs of the divine is extremely complicated; but in fact modern cultural morphologists are able to demonstrate that this symbolism is governed by a mere handful of laws; that it is capable of begetting mythological structures and rituals of identical form in cultures distinct from each other and having no historical links between them; and that it plays, according to circumstances, a liberating or oppressive role. Hence comes the view that the psycho-empirical material that various cultures use to elaborate their systems of sacred manifestations is of quite secondary importance. What does count is the use they make of this material; the important thing to observe is the fact that revelations of sacred mysteries are found everywhere, although, naturally, their shapes and forms vary from one culture to another. The history of religion, in even the most diverse geographical settings, always presents the divine as expressed through signs. The mystical is an *extracosmic* leap, a reaching beyond this world; and it is a prodigious manufacturer of symbols. It exists only when it is somehow expressed; and such is true even when its object is the eternal, in which case it first *consecrates* the things of time and space and makes of them objects that reveal the absolute. In this process we see the law that is common to every religion: man can get back to his beginnings only when he is content to take the indirect route of representations; he reaches the Infinite only by projecting it into finite objects, which become intermediaries of faith and instruments of worship.

Although the revelation of sacred mysteries always follows the way of representation, and even though the matter in which such a revelation is embodied has only a very relative importance when it is exercised in a pagan, that is to say, a naturalistic context, there is a complete change of meaning when the expression of the divine is centered directly on man. Hierophany (the revelation of sacred mysteries) and theophany (the appearance or manifestation of God in human form) become *anthropomorphic;* they cease being cosmic, that is, *phytomorphic,* and the gods take on the appearance of men; God becomes incarnate. And this is a real advance over naturalistic or fetishistic symbolisms.

However, religions can diverge on this very point. The divine can be humanized in two ways.

First, it can be expressed in the manner of Greek or Roman mythology; that is, by making gods out of legendary persons or even out of real persons (the theory of *euhemerism,* which in other respects is historically debatable). This results in a psychological pantheon in which the gods are actors who eternally play out the grandiose or childish dramas of human passions.

On the other hand, the divine may be expressed in human terms by taking as spokesmen, not fictitious beings lovingly elaborated by poets and artists, nor actual persons as divorced from their concrete relata, but rather historical characters, people of flesh and blood.

Such is the method of Hebrew mysticism. It does not regard as revelatory either external nature, as did the more ancient paganisms, or even the nature of man (in the psycho-rational sense), as did Graeco-Roman paganism. For the Jews history alone reveals God; only historical personages express the divine will through their actions.

How did it start? How was this unlooked-for historical consciousness produced in man? And why did it appear in the Jewish people? And why only among them?

It is not easy to answer these questions, and in any case the answer would demand much particularization. But one thing is sure—that, in discovering history as a social and religious category, Israel brought about remarkable things. First of all, it became aware of its unity; it saw the continuity of its efforts; it fixed aims and set tasks for itself; it even had the audacity to figure itself the center of man's destiny.

It did even more. To the great advantage of its own culture and of culture in general, it recovered the knowledge of origins—that with which every man is inextricably linked. By his very presence in the world man invests reality with significance, in such fashion that the world becomes a universe only through and in man's eyes; it becomes the occasion and material of history only through and in man's actions.

From this point of view, Judaism is a deliberate humanism, a humanism that attests that the world has not been given to man as a *natural* entity but as a *cultural* entity. As soon as nature presents itself to man, it is grasped in a human manner and is oriented towards humanity. Man appears as the great maker of sense and meaning, and the universe, so humanized, becomes the most radical, vast, and fruitful of institutions. No longer is history merely that which takes place on the world's stage; rather it is that which makes the world properly a human world. Nature raw is put to flight everywhere; nature itself becomes culture, that is to say, language, organization, efficiency. Such is the reason for Israel's being considered the discoverer of the positive character of law and ethics. Creation came from the hands of God, but Adam is its king.

Israel did not make this astounding discovery from worldliness but from motives of religion. This is a mark of the spirit of Israel. Man is the maker of history, and history reveals God's designs for the world, but only because God is the Invisible; because no one can look at His face and live; because God, who has neither mouth to speak nor hands to act, can speak and act only through His servants. *Prophecy,* in the broad sense, is the name given to this inevitable expression of the word of God by the men of God; *inspiration* means that the prophets, the sacred writers, are genuine "revealers," that they speak that which cannot be spoken and say that which cannot be said. Without them and without the community that first created their vocation and then ratified it, there would be no *acknowledged* expression of the divine. It is true that the community resisted for a long time before "acknowledging" the prophets, before accepting as authentic the oral or written messages of these religious geniuses. And it is also true that the community indulged the liberty of finding the word of God in the utterances of men who were foreigners to them. But these anomalies do not change the essence of the phenomenon of prophecy. Two things can be established in every case: first, a vision or grasp of the divine is formulated in a human testimony; second, a group of individuals—the Jewish people—accepted and gives value to this testimony by integrating it into its history. The category of *revelation* assumes both of these things: it presupposes that a witness of God *speaks* of God and that what he says about Him is *acknowledged* by others. Understood in this way, religious experience is not by any means a private revelation but is communication,

mutual verification, and collective research. In the ful-
lest sense there is no revelation except that which is
interpersonal and communal; this is all the better because
individual pronouncements about God are thus offered
or, at least, are retained only in relation to the history of
a people, only in connection with the traditions and
aspirations of a group.

The concept of revelation is often badly interpreted,
most likely because of the naive images that sometimes
attend it and the anthropomorphical formulas in which
it is frequently expressed. But such misinterpretation
confuses the content of a prophecy with the language
habits of a culture not much given to abstractions. Once
established, Jewish monotheism never allowed God to be
brought down to the level of man; yet it believed that
only man, as a participant in history, could voice the
thoughts of God. Judaism is essentially iconoclastic, a
religion without altars (except the one in the Temple)
and without images. It is founded on the strict interpretation of a book because that book lays out in historical perspective the destiny of the community, yet it forbids all material representations of God, and even forbids
the uttering of the name of God. Its sense of the ineffable
is acute.

And that is not all. It is precisely because the transcendence of "the God of all nations," the unique and
universal God, can never be brought into question that
anthropomorphism is able to explain Him without cari-
caturing Him. When it is well understood that God
cannot appear to men, that He cannot speak, that He
cannot become an object of sense experience, then there
is no danger in having Him appear, speak, and become

11

available to the senses. Here is the only way to enshrine and transmit in language that which surpasses all language. This process is unavoidable because man is incapable of experiencing anything without putting it into words. Each one of his experiences, including that of the sacred, must pass over into expression. Hence comes the strict paradox: because religious experience is experience of the invisible, *that is why* it is expressed in images. Religious experience is the experience of the inexpressible; *that is why* it is expressed in words. Of all religions Judaism is undoubtedly the one that used this rhetorical mechanism with the greatest precision. Yahweh is the hidden, inaccessible God, and that is why He became the approachable, ever-near God. He is the unseen God, impenetrable to the human mind; that is why He became the manifest God, revealed to man. These apparent contradictions are dialectical in nature and full of meaning. By His very nature, God is the Eternal, the Infinite, and is never on the same level as revelation or theophany which, in the context of history, are the signs or indications of His transcendence. Revelation *unveils* God because it expresses Him in terms of man, but at the same time it keeps Him *veiled*, because the signs it uses do not fix our attention on appearances. Instead, they direct us to look, through appearance, toward God's transcendence. The originality of Judaism consists in the very fact that it accepts as expressions of the divine only those that are incontestably of an *intentional* kind, namely, historical events and human actions. In this way it protects the category of revelation from all taint of idolatry and superstition, yet it does not make revelation a means of reducing or removing the mystery of the absolute, which remains undiminished. Although revelation allows man to discern and relate to a divine presence, it does not allow him to encompass or dominate it.

This *intentional* and human character of revelation flows logically from the attitude that Israel adopted toward history. The Jewish people took on themselves a religious mission and declared that they were God's chosen people because from the very beginning they were convinced that God manifests Himself only when humanity serves Him as a vehicle of expression. That is why Israel, in becoming God's herald, had the certainty that it was answering a call and following a vocation. They were to be preeminently the revealers and witnesses of the Eternal. Spurred on by this inspiration, the Jews believed that what *they* did, so long as they did it for God, *God* did. Thus their history assumed a revelatory value. It was no longer a mere assortment of actions, without connection or importance. It translated into human terms an action and a presence incomparably higher than anything human—the action and presence of the Creator, man's beginning and end. Therein lay divine revelation, even if that revelation took shape, as it had to, in human language and conduct with their inescapable limitations.

This way of infusing value into history gained strength from a dialectic that was proper to Judaism and that consisted, as I have said, in orienting nature by acting upon it. Nature in itself is not bad. Indeed, the Book of Genesis declares that all creation is good. And we know that Judaism, for this reason, never despised manual labor, whereas the pagan world regarded it as the task of slaves. Still, nature had been flawed by man's sin. When man lived in the Garden of Eden, in the paradigmatic age of the terrestrial paradise, he and nature were in perfect harmony; but in the present fallen condition of humanity, this harmony is broken. Man and the world are in a state of permanent hostility towards each other: suffering and death, the refractoriness of material things, the conflict of passions—these are the lot of fallen man. (The Christian teaching on Original Sin refers to this state.) Yet Jewish mysticism refuses to turn to pessimism even at the vision of this chaos. Instead, it charges chaos with meaning and thereby solves, with militancy and hope, what is referred to as the problem of evil. Men and the world are at war with each other— so be it! This is no reason for surrendering; rather, it is a reason for fighting. The goal to be reached is the final reconciliation of nature and mankind. This return of harmony and peace, this eschatological vision of a renewed world where, in the phrase of Isaiah, the wolf and the lamb will live peacefully together—this is what inspired and sustained the expectation of the Messiah. For the Jew, making history, giving it an aim, and working towards the coming of the Messiah are one and the same thing. Messianism is simply a program of action; it is a matter of finding meaning in history. This meaning consists in the progressive elimination of all the causes of division. Thus the living out of history is identical with the transformation of the world, aiming at a complete reorganization of its elements. This revolutionary character of Judaism is not at odds with its character as religion. Indeed, Israel knows that victory over nature is possible only if love of God and love of neighbor are put

14

into practice. Changing man's condition, redeeming or liberating him, is a *sacred* task. Perhaps this is the only instance of a religion that becomes more mystical the more it espouses the cause of history, which is to say, the establishment of man in the world.

Quite often this conception of history is oversimplified or even caricatured. The growth of Israel is represented as a succession of providential shocks, of disconcerting miracles. This is what happens when one allows oneself to fall into the trap of taking certain representations too literally. The memory of the Jewish people, like that of all other peoples, is idealistic and folkloristic. It moulds the past in terms of its current preoccupations and its future projects. Moreover, it has a taste for the magical, the "awe-inspiring": it takes pleasure in what is strange, even in what is "scandalous" (in the sense of salutary shock: see Hos. 1:1-7), and all this with a view to showing that God's ways are different from ours. The divine unexpectedness about which it speaks so lyrically has little to do with any voluntaristic theism, for this would amount to consecrating the arbitrary. Instead, the function of this biblical kind of history is to mark the break between the order created by man's free choice and the whole natural order. It does not destroy history on the human plane, but on the contrary, confirms it by restoring to it what is most properly and originally human.

This means that history is not the product of cosmic or biopsychical forces, as deterministic naturalism would have it. It is, instead, the result of initiatives that are free, effective, and capable of changing nature. But these initiatives are such only when they proceed from men unit-

15

ed with God and when they are used to carry out the principles of the Covenant between God and man. The intrigues of ambition, the dreams of conquest, the scheming of self-interest or pride—all are in vain. Only grace is efficacious. This is the message, this is the meaning of God's perpetual frustration of wholly human aims: pride-filled knowledge, rash hope in the accumulation of riches, the stability of political regimes, and the force of arms. Here too we see what is meant by the strength promised to weakness, the victory won in defeat, the reversal of fortune that comes about once confidence in God is substituted for confidence in self. The lesson to be drawn from the teaching of the Bible on divine providence is the radical opposition between that which succeeds in the order of nature and that which succeeds in the order of grace. Only oversight or a complete disregard for the context could lead one to see here, pushed to the limit, a kind of metaphysic of caprice. The fact that oversights and a disregard for context occur frequently is no reason for retaining them as sound rules of biblical interpretation; indeed, it is a good reason for thinking that the first rule of biblical interpretation ought to consist in excluding them.

Everything becomes clear once it is accepted that union with God is the ideal that guided all the actions of Israel and shaped its historical evolution. Every step, every event *has meaning:* they become stages in the long journey from the Covenant to the final reconciliation between man and nature. Even more: the Covenant throws light not only on what follows it but also on what preceded it. It allows us to retrieve the primordial events, the events of the paradigmatic epoch (the creation and the fall of man), and to reinsert them, now that their full meaning is plain, into the design of history. Then, but only then, does the Jew take stock both of all the defects and of the extent of his freedom. He knows that he can fulfill himself only by overcoming nature and by being receptive to grace. After all, for him history is only that daring enterprise that consists in mastering a rebellious world in order to establish in it a true republic of ends and aims, to set up what the Bible so expressively calls "the kingdom of God."

The danger of this concept is perhaps that of falling, now and then, into a merely human *meliorism.* Popular imagination is always prone to console itself for the mediocrity of the present by a vision of enchanting days ahead. Thus the hope of a Messiah can degenerate into an illusory *futurism;* it can become, in the secular domain, the expectation of material rewards, and this is the worst possible corruption of a spiritual ideal. In the religious sphere, it can become an alibi for real faith, as if earning salvation could be put off each day until tomorrow. However, these are errors or misunderstandings. Fanatics have used messianism as a weapon, while it has allowed the nonviolent to believe that a grace perpetually deferred must suffice for piety. But actually, the expectation of a Messiah meant something quite different. In fact, the monks of the desert, who were so numerous on the eve of our era, were able to restore its true meaning: messianism is indeed an expectation; it is also, however, a certitude. Salvation is not only to come, it is here now; there is an *Advent* of the heart, but it consists in being aware of the grace within. Like every other mysticism, Judaism has had a faulty memory; but

17

if it sometimes has forgotten its own lessons, no one can take from it the honor of having given those lessons.

Judaism has taught us what a historical religion is, and that is an invaluable heritage. Revelation given during the time and in the language of man is opposed to all naturalism. Salvation can come only from the decision to work upon nature, a decision and a work that draw their meaning and receive their effectiveness from the Covenant with God and from union with Him. The fruit of this union is called grace. Hence grace is really the motivating force of history; it sets the aim and allows it to be attained. It motivates human action, not only in order to modify the course of events, but literally to destroy it in order to re-create it—to destroy it on the natural plane where the forces of disassociation are continually warring, to re-create it under the divine sign of love, unity, and peace.

"Historical religion" means this effort of man, allied with God, to transmute nature, to make grace come into history and through history. In this sense salvation is never far off; it is already included in the act of offering oneself to God as a witness to His presence in the world. Israel invented the category of *history* on the day it understood that its vocation was to testify to the beyond in the here-and-now. But this vocation implied a particularly daring idea, namely, that the beyond finds no expression in the here-and-now except in the testimony of men among men. Because the Jewish people thought this thought and lived it, they are undoubtedly the ones who, of all the founders of religions, combined the greatest coherence with the extremest subtlety.

## Biblical Typology

Judaism is not only a historical religion but also a *typological* one: the latter attribute follows from the former—something that is rarely noted. Once it is agreed that history is revelatory and theophanic—inasmuch as men are privileged to express and enact divinity—then it must also be agreed that history is typological, so as to bring out its exemplary or normative character. Still, the term *typological* is used here in a general sense. Strictly speaking, a *type* exists only where one finds a clearly outlined model, a *figure* in a sufficiently concrete form, and in the purest cases, with a clearly individualized form. Furthermore, Israel accepts the condition that history is revelatory only when it expresses the Covenant with God. Now, in the eyes of Israel, this phenomenon exists in a unique context—the context of Israel. It is true that many tribes and other human groups have entered into a contract with their protecting gods, but Israel has always seen a fundamental difference between these alliances tainted with fetishism and polytheism, and her own alliance with Him who, in the person of Abraham, repudiates all paganism in order to adore the one God. That is why the Jewish people's covenant with the Most High is not simply a historical episode but is the very axis of history. It is therefore binding upon all humanity, which is called upon to recognize that revelation revolves about Judaism. Israel wished to be and believed itself to be the privileged witness, the "light to the nations." History thus became Judeo-centric in the same movement by which revelation became anthropocentric. Hence the care that the Jewish writers took, as early as the tenth century before Christ, to rewrite the history of

19

Israel so that it would serve as a model for all nations.

It is possible to see here a progressive narrowing of the concept of typology. The expression-type of the divine is first of all history, in the large sense, and not nature. This interpretation corresponds, if you will, to God's covenant with Noah, who represents humanity saved from the Flood. The expression-type of the divine is, next, in a more restricted yet more precise sense, the history of Israel, which corresponds to the covenant that God made with Abraham, the father of all believers. At this stage, only the Jewish people possesses revelation, and only the history of the Jews is the figure, the *type,* of salvation. Nevertheless, the meaning of the typology does not terminate here: it becomes richer in intension as its extension narrows. Experience teaches that it is foolish to expect the same exemplary conduct from every individual member of a nation and to the same degree without distinction. Experience shows us that the masses are forgetful, lazy, and slow to change; that their moments of fervor and enthusiasm are short; and that, in addition, they are more likely to become infatuated with what flatters and beguiles them than with what demands effort. The Jewish people claimed to be God's chosen, yet the majority slipped into idolatry with an astounding mindlessness. They were continually having to be called to order and led back to the narrow path of Mosaic monotheism. Accordingly, they needed teachers, guides, and leaders, who were unflinching and clear-sighted. To put it another way, only an elite was able to conduct them on the right path and keep them from straying. While the mass of the Jewish people allow themselves to be corrupted, only a small number, the "remnant of

Israel," remain capable of saving them. Revelation, for this reason, finally becomes concentrated in the testimony of a few, who then become the "type" of what has to be believed and done.

Their typicality is twofold: it can be seen on the plane of *history* and on the plane of *spirituality*. From the point of view of *history*, these exemplars mark the stages of Israel's achievement of self-consciousness. They form a succession of landmarks in that progress. At that epoch and in those circumstances, they represent the attitude that enables the people of God to stay faithful to their vocation. That is why their example remains in every epoch a model for imitation; and their existence as types, valid in the past, still retains its value as teaching for the present. Thanks to Holy Scripture, which has recorded the steps of their progress and, moreover, has turned them into eloquent paradigms, the Israelite community can, in them, recognize itself and see more clearly its destiny.

From the *spiritual* point of view, it is no longer just the collectivity whose destined path in history is lighted up by the example of these men; it is each individual, each religious soul, who can profit by their attitude and adopt it in his own life. Yet this imitation must not be servile and mechanical. It is practically impossible to copy unchanged the actions of people who lived in very different circumstances. It is a question, rather, of reproducing an attitude in an active and personal way, of following a style of life, a type of existence that preserves its relevance at every moment to whoever adopts it, no matter how little he understands how to adapt it. Taken in this sense, biblical typology is not mere slavish conformity to a preexistent model. It is rather the transformation of oneself which occurs at the exact moment when the decision to change one's life marries by an act of free choice an exemplary mode of life, which one knows to be an incarnation of the ideal.

In addition, the historical and spiritual points of view are linked together, since for Israel the same values shape collective and individual salvation. The values that emerged at one point of time as a result of the initiative of a few individuals cannot be brought into question. They are a definitive acquisition from which each one should profit, and not to acknowledge them would be to regress. The street of progress is one way. And this notion is an incomparable benefit. By having recourse to Scripture, each believer can begin at once building at the highest level of past achievements; and in his spiritual life he can immediately reap the advantage of long experience. From generation to generation, capital has been accumulating, so that the latest arrivals, if they only know how to use the knowledge, are always more advanced than those who went before them. The "types" presented to them by tradition are not confining shackles but are instead the occasion and the assurance of undeniable personal advancement.

One begins to see how well Judaism has been served by typology. The Israelite community did not paint portraits after the manner of the moralist who seeks to edify and who therefore creates his models of conduct to illustrate the lessons he intends to teach. No. the Jews went about the matter in a less abstract way: they recognized the face of their destiny and vocation in certain chosen men; even more, they saw that these men were God's special witnesses, envoys, and messengers; and that is why the Jews turned them into types, typified them. But they did so only because the lives of these men were already, in themselves, *typical,* which is to say, exemplary.

The Jews also accepted exemplary characters of an inferior kind, such as the heroes of apologues and fables. But these are the exception, and the vast majority of the biblical types are truly historical, and all of them involve an awareness of history.

Similarly, the Jewish community made exemplars of visionary or anticipatory beings such as the man of sorrows described by Isaiah and the son of man of whom Daniel spoke. But it is significant that this prophetic, eschatological typification was truly fixed only when, much later, it crystallized about a historic Messiah (Jesus). In rabbinical exegesis this typification meant only the personification of the people of Israel, "the servant of God" in Isaiah, and "the people of the saints" of the Most High, in Daniel. These are instances of the rather common practice of typifying the collectivity in an individual and according to some customary formula in order to illuminate a historical situation.

And finally, as the typology of the Jewish community became complicated and its familiar "figures" multiplied, it produced proportionately many that appear completely unreal and enigmatic. Those special forms of literature, prophecy, and even more, apocalypse, occasionally involve such a tangle of facts and dreams, memories and predictions that it becomes impossible to establish which is which. But a close analysis of images and ideas is of less importance here than the total effect that the writers wished to create. After all, it is possible that the main purpose of these literary pieces may have been to serve as a mirror for the religious imagination: by putting into them what he was seeking, every man could find himself there, contemplate himself there. Polyvalent meaning is sometimes a trap, but in this case it is an inexhaustible store of riches. The prophetic and apocalyptic genres would not have been cultivated so enthusiastically if they had not answered a need both in the authors and in the readers. But it is significant that even these modes of expression remain tied to events, to current problems, live conflicts, and imagined solutions. The obscure and tortuous typology that the Jews employed is in this way still firmly linked to a historical basis. It is, moreover, continuous with the most ancient typology, which it constantly recalls and remolds.

During the Diaspora, when the Jews came across principles of interpretation different from their own, Greek allegory, for example, they were able to use them in their turn and to give them an appreciably different slant (see Proverbs, Wisdom). St. Paul and St. John, the author of the fourth Gospel, profited by the lessons of allegory, and even more so, the Greek Fathers when they came to interpret the Bible; hence the tendency of modern authors to treat Jewish typology in a plainly ahistorical fashion.

Yet to proceed in this way is to depart far from the original meaning of Jewish typology, which even the most allegorizing of the New Testament authors or the Fathers were very careful never to obscure. Thus one can make the Garden of Eden, the Flood, or the Exodus a figure of various aspects of the spiritual kingdom that is to come; but, according to Jewish canons, the parallel holds only if the types chosen are related to the place they occupy in Israel's consciousness throughout the course of her history. And even then such an approach can be enlightening only to the extent it places in the foreground, not the quaint elements in the different narratives, but the characters central to them: Adam, Noah, Moses—*these* are the true types and the bearers of knowledge, not the material of fabulous invention or reconstruction, which is there only to lend personal characterization. The attitudes of these men are first in importance. It is owing to these attitudes that we can not only learn something about our destiny but also assume the dispositions that will enable us to realize that destiny. It is in this connection that biblical typology seems to be charged with an exemplary quality, with efficacious examples, but not at all in the order of metaphor, of simple comparison, or of episodic recollection. Rather it is on the plane of the example given and lived, of the example that engenders a value and urges one on to re-engender it unceasingly in daily life. Biblical literature gives no learned definition of sin, justice, faith, sacrifice, or patience under trial; and only rarely and exceptionally do abstract truths obtrude upon its narrative. Abruptly and spontaneously it brings the heroes of its history on stage (Adam, Abraham, Isaac, Moses, David, Job, and so on); and it matters little here whether biblical literature is dealing in true history or in myth (for example, the account of man's origin), since even mythical history was formed in time and reveals qualities of the Jewish soul. There is a special art involved here, in elaborating religion in history, of thinking out the ethical and the mystical in

25

concrete situations, and only in such situations.

If we wish to put typology to the test of truth, obviously we must cease to regard the Bible as a comic book for children, or as a packet of colored postcards. At first glance one is tempted to believe that typification is a proof that biblical literature is incapable of presenting or arriving at general ideas as such, that it is confined to generalizing from particular cases. But this would be to misjudge it badly. It is the natural tendency of biblical literature to refuse to propound the general apart from the particular. But at the same time, it strives for an authentic and immediate grasp of the universal idea as well as of the singular instance. Abraham was ready to immolate his son out of obedience, and he is the type of absolute self-sacrifice. His example incarnates the idea, but this is not to say that the validity of the idea depends strictly upon the example, because in that case the idea would be true only under the conditions in which Abraham acted. Even if it were generalized, the example would be of scant value. If the truth of the example is to be unlocked, its particularities must appear as relative and contingent; and only the meaning it conveys and its exemplary character are to be seen as having the qualities of necessity and universality. Thus the meaning and the exemplary idea are justified in and by themselves, independently of the circumstances in which, on that one occasion, they appeared.

We see that typology is a shrewd, if unlearned, way of showing the universal directly in the particular. The superficial commentator gets the impression of a mode of thought that is only able to cope with the particular, but which, nevertheless, is able to force a variety of meanings out of it. This kind of interpretation is reminiscent of Berkeley's "general idea," that is to say, a particular idea that has infinitely varied applications. Yet typology is not a negation of the universal. At most, it denies that the universal can be perceived other than in what is expressed, which is always particular and even ambiguous. In our day, phenomenology has developed an analogous thesis: that is why it entertains no hostility, but rather the contrary, towards the typologies it finds in sociology, in ethnography, and in the history of religions.

## Concrete Universality

Our development of the relationship between the universal and the particular has led us almost imperceptibly to the third point, namely, that Judaism is a *universal* religion, although one that is confined to a *particular* mode of expression.

It is universal at least in intention since it adores the one God who rules over all creation and who must save all men. Judaism was, in large measure, truly universal, although there is a tendency to forget the fact. Thanks to the Jews of the Diaspora, who quickly became more numerous than those who remained in Palestine, Judaism finally accepted pagan converts. Even before the Christian era, it offered the pagans two formulas for conversion: *proselytism,* which involved circumcision and the strict observance of the liturgical calendar, and the program for *"those who feared God,"* which allowed candidates to remain uncircumcised but expected them to be faithful to the great lessons of the Scriptures and to certain practices. By thus admitting pagans, Judaism showed that it was capable of going beyond all sectarian-

27

ism of race or education. It worked loyally for the conversion of all nations and wanted the God of Abraham to be recognized everywhere as the God of the whole human race.

Yet Judaism never understood universal access in any other way than through the observance of particular laws. Every man had the opportunity to adopt the faith of Israel, but only on one condition—that he subscribe to the Covenant, that he become a Jew in spirit, and that he submit to the Law, at least in essentials. And he was not fully assimilated unless he accepted the Law as a whole—circumcision, rest on the Sabbath, reading the Torah, and so on. These were precise requirements and they demanded great adaptability and sacrifice on the part of any pagan who wished to become a convert. By mitigating these conditions the Jews could have obtained a more rapid and complete success, but certain minimum obligations were always maintained; and this attitude of requiring positive commitment, the adherence to particcular rules, is not an accidental, but rather an essential, feature of Judaism.

This characteristic of Judaism appears in various ways. First, it is seen in the principle of historical revelation: if God is transcendent, if He does not speak, if human testimony alone transmits "the word of God," it follows that the revealed "word" must correspond with a particular teaching. Second, the characteristic appears in the application of the principle of historical revelation: God's witnesses are men who belong to an ethnic, social, and cultural group; their history is made up of a thousand special items. Third, and very importantly, in the case of Judaism the foundation of its insti-

tutions lies less in a political pact subject to all kinds of
vicissitudes than in a religious vow, a Covenant, that
commands a position superior to all material upheavals.

Israel was thus led to adopt a mode of life which
would be proof against every trial. Even without a
country, without a state, the people of God remained a
nation. Their success came about from the recollection of
their origins, of their vocation, and they had an infallible
means for making this recollection possible, namely, the
written Law. It was by the Law, and by the Law alone,
that the Jews were able to hold on, despite their being ex-
iled and scattered over the face of the earth, despite their
being deprived of their own territory, of any political ap-
paratus, and even of the language of their fathers during
the Hellenistic period. They owed their temporal salvation
to one thing alone, their sacred historical literature. It was
their good fortune to have possessed a scriptural religion,
something that has not been given to all peoples. But this
religion based on texts, this religion formalized by the
scribes, was by that very fact extremely particularized. It
is inevitable that cultures that express themselves in writ-
ing sedimentate more quickly than others, something that
is at once an advantage and a liability. It is an advantage
insofar as continuity is better assured, control is easier,
and communication more widely diffused; but it is a
liability because the letter of the law, which sustains
memory, may threaten the spirit of the law and foster the
illusion that formula can substitute for value.

Israel was conscious of both the largeness and the
limitations of Scripture. It was a religion of the inspired
Book, to the point of finding under the veil of words the
presence of God. But Israel was also capable of com-

menting upon the Book, interpreting it, and even, until the redaction of Esdras (398 B.C.), rewriting it. Unceasingly, the Jews kept their sacred scriptures vivid and relevant by oral glosses. Tradition, having dictated the books of Scripture, never feared that its own contribution risked exhaustion or replacement by the written word. That is why Scripture was, all things considered, beneficial and liberating. Without the Bible, the Jews would sooner or later have lost their conviction that they were God's chosen race, which is the same as saying that they would have lost their reason for living. The Bible constantly reminded them of their history, and they needed that reminder while foreigners were their masters, which was most of the time. The Bible also preserved for the Jews throughout the centuries a collection of prayers, a discipline of worship, which kept their practice of religion uniform, even though they lacked any dogmatic structure properly so called. To the modern mind this state of affairs is unusual and even surprising, for here we have a spiritual authority which makes faith revolve around a living liturgy and a strict adherence to the letter of a law, but which excludes every ideology founded on logical argumentation.

We have a revelation immanent in history, a history reduced to the story of a nation, a nation defined by a religious vocation, and this vocation inscribed in the text of a book—is not this the triumph of particularism? Actually, it is not, because this particularism implies and affirms a universal aim. Judaism is, indeed, a paradoxical religion because it teaches that the unique and universal God revealed Himself to a desert tribe, that the whole of hu-

manity will be saved through the witness of this tribe, a
nation without frontiers, that the message of this nation,
contained in a book of about a thousand pages, is capable
of forming the conscience of every individual and every
people. These simple, yet daring, contentions upset
the classical antinomies—immanence and transcendence,
nationalism and internationalism, literalness and freedom. The audacity of Judaism is contained in a few
propositions: the transcendent is accessible only through
the immanent; the universal is attained only through the
particular; although the letter may kill and the spirit
give life, only the spirit of the letter kindles the spirit of
man.

Stated in this way, these contrasts appear self-
evident, yet few men are ready to accept them intellec-
tually and live according to them. A phenomenology of
institution can at least make the effort to show the strict-
ness of these propositions and to follow out their implications, for the proper function of every institution is
to bring the ideal and the real into harmony, to unite the
indefiniteness of a theoretical duty with the definiteness
of a concrete duty. Yet only religious institution claims
to reconcile the infinite and the finite, the absolute of the
spirit and the relativity of history. Judaism undertook
this reconciliation resolutely and deliberately and it did
not fail, for it gained adherents and led the way. From it
Christianity borrowed the institutional principle, modi-
fying many of the particular features of the Hebrew
religion but reconciling the particular and the universal
in its own way. This characteristic opposition has been
incorporated by Christianity into the very idea of institution; and if it has accomplished the task well in fact,

it is only because it has accomplished it by right and law. But to follow this line of thought would lead us too far afield, to the very sources of the Law and of all human devising. In the process phenomenology would need to transcend its own limits and become a subject-object philosophy. Suffice it to say that positive Christian religion, which is a replica of the Jewish model, attests at least to the insufficiently recognized fact, that Israel was, as much as the Greek philosophers and the Roman jurists, the founder of the West.

# 3. The Christian Institution

Belief in Jesus Christ came into being in Palestine about the year 30 of our era, in a Jewish milieu—which was very much a mixed milieu, for at that time a number of Jewish sects flourished there.

The Sadducees were aristocrats and conservatives, who held only those doctrines that had appeared before the Babylonian Captivity and the Persian domination (about the sixth century before Christ).

The Pharisees were impassioned believers whose fervor sometimes drove them to excesses; but at least they had the merit of professing a personal religion.

The Essenes and similar groups of every shade of belief (for example, the different baptizing communities) lived according to the spirituality of the desert, did not take part in the worship of the Temple in Jerusalem, and had their own rites and mystical doctrine, in which Pythagorean and even Iranian influences can be detected. Above all, they were convinced that the last period of the world had arrived, the time when the promise God had made to Abraham would be fulfilled, namely, that Israel would be a great nation and would impose its Law on the whole earth, thus assuring its own salvation and that of mankind.

Finally, the Zealots were members of a resistance group who opposed the Roman occupation of Palestine. They did not hesitate to use violence and specialized in assassinating Roman officials and soldiers.

All of these groups were exposed to the influence of an apocalyptic literature, which disturbed some and inflamed others with zeal because it announced that the Messiah, the Son of David, was soon to appear and restore the kingdom of God, that is, the sovereignty of Israel. The prudent folk, those of some status, were warily on guard scenting the danger of subversion; but ardent men, the patriots, believed that the liberation of their country was near, whereas religious souls had an increasing presentiment that the kingdom of God might not be a kingdom of this world. In any case, the Messianic idea haunted men's minds and tended more and more to be embodied in a liberator, a savior, in the style of the Book of Daniel and that of Enoch. The group formed by Jesus and His disciples was permeated by this kind of thought and seemed to be but one Messianic community among others. Far from being an oddity in contemporary Judaism, it resembled all the sects that revivified the great tradition of prophetic inspiration and found a spiritual program in Messianism.

We cannot here retrace the history of this group; moreover, it is very difficult to reconstruct it in detail. The Gospels are books of faith and not scientific works: they indicate a religious judgment on the life and death of Jesus; and their aim is not to satisfy profane curiosity, even when, as in the Gospel of St. Luke, special care was taken to be precisely accurate and to check the facts. We take it for granted that the reader is familiar, at least in broad outline, with events reported in the New Testament (which is so called in contrast to the Jewish Bible or Old Testament); and therefore we shall not try to repeat the work of the historians. Nevertheless, we must emphasize the point that these very facts, of which the historical basis is admitted by most critics, are facts that have been elaborated by faith, in the sense that religious instruction has already worked over the events and declared their religious meaning. Thus it is easier to draw from these facts a phenomenology of Christian *meanings* than a historical reconstruction; at least if one understands this latter term to mean a scientific verification apart from the perspectives of religion.

This being said, we may ask, What do we find in the original synthesis of *facts and doctrine* which the New Testament—the four Gospels, the Acts of the Apostles, the Epistles, and so on—presents? The answer is that we find there a transposition of the principal Jewish structures, and it is in this connection that emergent Christianity was a Judaism before it evolved in a Graeco-Roman environment. The Jewish context described at the beginning of this chapter is almost entirely reflected in nascent Christianity; in any case, it is sufficient to confront the Christian institution with the three fundamental propositions of Judaism (see p. 6ff.) to establish that Christianity made them her own, that she received and respected them, even if she did treat them in a new way.

This exercise in confrontation will not permit us to pass in review all the Christian categories, but it will surely give us the chance to highlight the essential elements.

## Messianism Fulfilled

Christianity, like Judaism, is a historical religion.

In this regard, it confines itself to reiterating and as-similating the lesson of the Jewish Bible. It adopts the idea of a divine revelation through the history of the Jews. It ratifies the idea of a chosen race and enters the general scheme of the Covenant. Likewise, it makes use of the myth of Genesis and, with St. Paul, it even adduces a new exegesis of the texts concerning the fall of man. All the more readily, it accepted with fervor the heritage of the prophets and nourished its prayer-life at the well-springs of the Psalms. In a general way we can say that Christianity, like Judaism and *insofar as it is a Judaism,* is a religion of the Book. In fact, from the very begin-ning, the apostolic community restricted itself to repeat-ing the lessons of the Old Testament (the New Testament had not yet been written); and it was sufficient for it to be able to apply the prophecies to its Master.

But was Christianity only a Jewish sect? Yes, and no. Yes, in the sense that for many years it did not break with Judaism, to which it owed its first concepts, its first rites, although both bore the mark of an Es-senian Judaism rather than of the static Judaism of the priests of Jerusalem and doctors of the Law. Neverthe-less, Christianity was *not* a Jewish sect, because even the most Judaizing Christianity (for example, that which was personified in James, "the brother of the Lord," as op-posed to the Judeo-Hellenic Christianity of St. Paul) was already an original creation.

But in what did this creation consist? In the fact that the disciples of Jesus, without repudiating Jewish monotheism, suddenly had a new focus of doctrine and worship—the risen Christ. Already the adherents of the New Covenant (no doubt one of the branches of the Essenian brotherhood) had exalted one of their leaders, the all-holy Master, who had been put to death by the high priests and glorified by God. Thus faith in the Christ of glory did not appear as a unique and unnatural initiative in the Judaism of the period. Hence we can understand why the first Christian community did not immediately seem heterodox or schismatic to those who saw it emerge. For example, the Resurrection of Christ had analogies, even though analogies do not account for it. The important thing to note is that faith in Christ, although it did not run counter to certain forms of contemporary Judaism, was a specific orientation; and that, although the people of the time were scarcely aware of what was happening, the new religion was gradually to change the tone and the nature of Messianic spirituality. And that is the decisive point.

First of all, Christianity gave a name to the hitherto anonymous Messiah for whom pious Jews had been waiting, and immediately the prophecies of the Scriptures were focussed on this Messiah, who had finally been identified. Then, by proclaiming that God had visited His people and that the day of the Emmanuel had dawned on Israel, Christianity arrested eschatological hope in full flight and turned it into joy and certitude, with the result that prophetical futurism was definitively and radically transformed into the actuality of salvation. True, many traces of eschatology remained in the New Testament, and belief in the *Parousia,* the return of Christ in glory for the solemn restoration of the kingdom, persisted breathlessly for one or two generations. But this was, so to speak, an effect of the speed with which hope had changed to certainty. Henceforth, the center of gravity of religion was elsewhere, in the conviction that the Messiah was no longer merely to be expected but that He had already appeared in the person of Jesus, and this was to cause the dwindling of Judaism.

Official Judaism remains, in fact, a Messianism whose due date is open; Christianity, on the other hand, is a Messianism that has come to term and been paid off. In the same way, Judaism clings to a revelation that is still unfolding in history and that will end only with the world. Revelation will only be fully achieved in the next world. Christianity, on the contrary, limits and interrupts revelation within history and regards it as having come to an end with the death of the last direct witness of the Messianic events. For the Christian, the "last days" have already begun, expectancy has ceased, and salvation is coupled with the present. Christianity does keep its eyes fixed on the next world and speaks, in its turn, about hope, but it does so in the perspective of an afterlife. To put it another way, Christianity adds an eschatology of death and of eternal happiness to the certainty that, even here below, grace is superabundant. And it holds that the glory of the next world will be the flowering of this grace and that it will not be a different grace. Thus we are dealing with a Messianism fulfilled at a point in space and at a moment in time, and this Messianism involves an actuality of personal salvation which allows the Christian to feel that he is redeemed and delivered by his faith *hic et nunc*. These two points effect more than a shift of accent with regard to Judaism. Instead, they are equivalent to the reversal of a trend which dates from the identification of Jesus Christ as the Messiah, for being able to name the Messiah and recognizing that salvation is here and now are the same thing.

## Christological Typification

This modification of Judaism was not immediately perceptible because the new form of worship continued to speak the language of traditional Judaism. Although it daily increased in strength, the Christian faith still had recourse to the biblical modes of thought in formulating its doctrine. The new religion borrowed from the old even for the purpose of differentiating itself. This process is seen in the manner in which the first Christian community exerted itself to "typify" the person of Jesus. In doing so, it consciously obeyed the laws of Jewish typology. At the same time it was unconsciously ensuring the best prospects for the object of its belief, because it vowed itself to a reverence for its Master and gauged the meaning of Christology—no matter how much development it should undergo—by the devotion to Him. Thus the choice of Master and Exemplar included a rule of great benefit in that it required the maintenance of this positive relationship, and thereby prevented Christianity from turning into several religions as it was relayed through successive cultures.

There is no better proof of the Jewish descent of Christianity than this use of biblical typology in respect to Jesus. At the start, it was as if the Christian faith were recognizing in Jesus the existence of a type, a prophetic and revelatory role in the received sense of these ideas among the Jews. But a forward movement of renewal occurred, inasmuch as this typification took place in the light of the fulfilled Promise. And the type of the Messiah, according to which the life and death of Christ were to be described, very quickly showed an astonishing fecundity, for it not only summed up all that the prophets Isaiah, Jeremiah, Ezekiel, Daniel, and others, had to say about the Messiah, but it even went so far as to enrich itsself with contributions from non-Jewish sources. Not confining itself to Hebrew structures alone, it received considerable impetus from a penetration of the broader cultural milieu of Judeo-Hellenism. To put it another way: Christianity was so far from repudiating the principle of Jewish typology as to make it bear fruit in other contexts of civilzation, an expansion that showed, not the inability of the Semitic mind to express everything needful, but rather its exceptional plasticity. People believe too readily that messianic typology was foredoomed to failure in the conquest of the Gentile world. But this is not entirely correct: messianic typology may appear to have had its limitations, but what kind of thing has not? In many ways, it showed remarkable flexibility and adaptability, yet never ceased to preserve its primary meaning. In reshaping messianic typology, while spreading it abroad, Judeo-Hellenism ran the risk of pollution; yet a new profundity accrued to it and not distortion, even as it was superimposed upon the most diverse cultures. This is one of the best examples of conceptual vitality to be found in the history of religions; and it will be well worth our while to review this process, at least briefly. For the sake of convenience, we shall mark out seven stages of Christology.

1. Even while Jesus was alive, the apostles formed a group whose religious life, as we have seen, was of Messianic inspiration. Jesus Himself had to have recourse to

the concept of the Messiah to define His vocation, and, as certain exegetes believe, there is nothing against the opinion that meditation on the prophecies of Isaiah may have disposed Him to conceive His role as Messiah, not as glorious, but as sorrowful, or more pertinently, as glorious because it was sorrowful. At this stage, Jesus is the Messiah in the sense of the prophecies. It is not surprising that the apostles should have held this belief, at least after prolonged contact with Him. The astonishing thing is rather that they continued to believe that He was invested with the messianic attributes, despite the Crucifixion. In short, the miracle does not consist in the Messianism of the Galilean Master, but in the posthumous Messianism of the Crucified.

2. If Christ's disciples had not believed in His Resurrection, they could never have withstood the severe test of Calvary, as the episode of the disciples of Emmaus forcefully implies (Luke 24:13-35). Here the religious leap was more daring and demanding than the apologetic of the empty tomb, for one had to believe, all at once and without tangible evidence (there were no eyewitnesses to the Resurrection), that the defeat of the Master was not final, that since death was the wages of sin and since Jesus had led the life of a just man, death had no power to keep Him in thrall. Hence He had not been destroyed by death but had, on the contrary, conquered it and was alive again and glorified, which, in the anthropological style of the era, was expressed by saying that He had risen from the dead. This conclusion owed little to abstract logic, and no doubt, would not have been compelling if it had not been corroborated by instances of

41

Christophany, that is, of visions of the Risen Lord. All the Gospels emphasize these appearances of Christ, and it is possible that Christophanic emotions nourished the great Paschal enthusiasm. St. Paul himself said that he had been granted an analogous favor, which had been decisive in his conversion.

Only those who regard man's spirituality as a mere biological function and who refuse to accept the concept of resurrection as indicative of an afterlife can allow themselves to regard belief in the Resurrection of Christ as illusory and deceptive. In proclaiming that Jesus was truly risen from the dead, the Christian faith was simply accepting in a typical case what it anticipated for mankind in general, as St. Paul himself explained very clearly (1 Cor. 15:12-32). But such is not our problem here, and all discussion on the deep truth of the Resurrection is better left to the schools of metaphysics.

From the time of the Resurrection, the messianic belief of the apostles was illuminated, transfigured. St. Peter proclaimed: "Jesus of Nazareth, a man attested to you by God . . . , you crucified. . . . But God raised him up, having loosed the pangs of death. . . . God has made him both Lord and Christ, this Jesus whom you crucified" (Acts 2:22-36). In this text the crucified Jesus owed to His being raised from the dead by God the double title of "Lord" and "Christ." Thus the type of the Messiah now connotes not only the prophetic attribute of revelation, but also the sacral and worshipful attribute of lordship. Henceforth He is the glorious Christ, even though, in the chronological scheme of the liturgy, it is the Ascension that marks His great return to the Father. And He is glorious because He has suffered although He was

42

innocent, and so "God raised him up, having loosed the pangs of death, because it was not possible for him to be held by it" (Acts 2:24). Thus the Passion of Christ is placed under the sign of the Resurrection, and the Cross is interpreted and *given value* in the light of Easter. The Messianism of Jesus is confirmed, but at the same time it changes its scope: the prophet is recognized as the Lord, and He is established in that mystical sphere in which the homage of faith and the appeal of prayer can swiftly reach Him as the Divine Mediator, the High Priest—according to the language of the Epistle to the Hebrews (7:24-28; 9:11-15).

3. To the deacon Stephen, who was stoned to death while Paul the Pharisee looked on, we owe the development of a new stage in Christology. Stephen was condemned to death by the Sanhedrin because of his reforming zeal. He had criticised the worship in the Temple, reproached the Jewish people with their chronic opposition to the Holy Spirit, and charged them with the crime of executing Jesus. At the same time, according to the text of the Acts of the Apostles (7:37-57), he showed clearly how the Passion had made the prophet who so resembled Moses, the "just man betrayed," into the very type of the Son of Man described by Daniel. Thus understood, the Messiah was the judge sent by God, He who was to come in glory to punish the wicked and inaugurate an "everlasting dominion" (Dan. 7:13-14). Once more, passing through suffering and death enabled Jesus to transcend the human condition. Further, if Stephen's prayer to the "Lord Jesus" (Acts 7:59) is authentic, it proves that the Messiah was then the direct object of de-

votion, that piety had become Christocentric. The Messianism of Jesus had come full circle: He who had announced the Kingdom had now become the subject of that announcement; He had shown God to people, and they now discovered God in Him.

4. The Christology of St. Paul extended and surpassed that of Stephen. In his epistles, St. Paul made little reference to the details of the life of Christ but concentrated all his attention on the two terms, "crucifixion" and "resurrection." Like Stephen, he understood that the Temple sacrifices were a form of worship no longer valid, since Jesus had expiated the sins of men once and for all upon the Cross. It was, therefore, sufficient to associate oneself with His sacrifice, to be crucified with Him, to die with Him, in order to rise like Him (Rom. 6:4-9). For Paul, Christological typology here played the role of an exemplarism that was both historical and suprahistorical at the same time.

It was historical because the crucifixion on Golgotha had shed the blood of Christ (Eph. 2:16); it was suprahistorical because Christ's attitude of oblation—His voluntary sacrifice, His obedience unto death, the degrading death of crucifixion, had a meaning and an influence that reached far beyond the event (Phil. 2:8-11). It is eternally true and eternally efficacious that the immolation of the just man saves sinners (Eph. 5:2; Rom. 5:6-8), and that only such an immolation can save them.

To sustain this idea, St. Paul introduced the figure of the paschal lamb, with finer and more delicate features than the symbolic scapegoat. But it is essential to understand fully this mythic of substitution. If it means that the innocent are to be struck down in place of the guilty, it merely combines the arbitrary with the hateful; and salvation is won entirely apart from just those people who need to be saved. It must be understood, *through* and *beyond* the image, that the sacrifice of the "spotless victim" is the only one that can have expiatory value. It destroys sin, not by repentance, which remains impure, but by total disinterestedness, absolute faith, and unmixed love. Literally, it is grace in action: it is not inspired by any egotistical aim, and by definition, it is unmotivated and entirely gratuitous. It is the gift of self, charity without restriction, perfect union with the God of Holiness. That is why the Passion appears as the type of the working out of salvation. That is why men are saved by cleaving to the exemplary offering and death of Christ, by imitating Him to the point of adopting His attitudes (Gal. 3:27), to the point of living with His life (Gal. 2: 20). On the other hand, works of the Law cannot give true salvation, for they remain inadequate, extrinsic, ambiguous (Gal. 2:10-14; Rom. 4:13-16). Only the acts and attitudes of Christ have revelatory and normative value; and this value they have in what must be called a sacramental sense, since they contain and communicate grace. St. Paul was conscious of this when he called the rite of the Lord's Supper the memorial of Calvary, and even more than a memorial, an active and personal participation in the "new covenant" (1 Cor. 10:16-17; 11:23-29).

St. Paul's Christology is not solely soteriological in essence, that is to say, it does not refer only to Christ's redemption of man; and, at times, it takes on a singularly daring theological aspect. For St. Paul, Christ is "the image of the invisible God, the firstborn of all creation. . . .

All things were created through him and for him. He is before all things, and in Him all things hold together" (Col. 1:15-17). Further, Christ is a divine being who existed before His manifestation to the world and who, in order to show Himself in human form, had to renounce His divine condition (Phil. 2:6-7). These texts, which are difficult to interpret, at least prove that, for St. Paul, the Messiah was no longer only of a royal or lordly type (in accordance with the prevailing tone of Messianism after the foundation of the monarchy in Israel), but of a "sapiential" type. In other words, St. Paul typified Christ in the manner of the Book of Proverbs and the Book of Wisdom. By progressing along this path, Christian thought was to allow the Greek world to reap the full benefit of Davidic or prophetic Messianism.

Some have seen in this innovation a threat to Yahwistic monotheism, but their fear is not well-founded, because St. Paul himself subordinates Christ to God (1 Cor. 15:27-28). Having sifted through some quite complicated gnostic systems, St. Paul seeks to place Christ on a transcendent plane while being careful not to do any injury to monotheistic faith. Sapiential typology suggests that Christ is "the image of the invisible God," the prototype of creation. This terminology allows St. Paul to reconcile opposites: on the one hand, God and His "image" are distinct from each other, in the sense that one is expressed and the other expresses; on the other hand, they are one, because the "image," in order to be a faithful expression, must reflect the plenitude of God (Col. 1:19). These intuitions were to pour clearer at the hands of Greek intellectuals. But there is no authority for saying that Pauline theology was in any way non-monotheistic. It was inevitable that he should try to define the bond between Christ the Mediator, Christ the Savior, with God; and it is normal that he should have used for this purpose a theory of expression that falls back on the biblical ideas of creation, of image (in the sense of *figure* or *type),* as the author of the Epistle to the Hebrews (1:3) expressly did.

5. The fourth Gospel pursues the same line of thought, but we find there a concept that is more adequate for expressing the preexistence or eternity of Christ. In the very prologue, Jesus is presented as the incarnate *Logos.* The application of this term to Christ is clear evidence that the author was a Hellenized Jew, because only an Israelite of the Diaspora could have mastered both the Jewish and Greek cultures. At all events, the choice of word was a happy one. For a Jew, *logos* recalls *davar,* "the word," taken here as the word of God; for a Greek, it recalls the doctrine of Philo of Alexandria. Thus it is understood by each in his own language, a curious example of *glossolalia,* the miraculous gift of tongues, which allows two idioms, two mentalities, to combine without losing their original quality.

In giving Jesus the title of *Logos,* in declaring that the *Logos* abides in God from all eternity and that He is God-made-man, the fourth Gospel brought the *type* of the Messiah to the realm of the absolute, raising it directly to the height of the Divinity. Not that John confuses God with His envoy, the Father with the Son. On the contrary, like St. Paul, he always distinguishes between them: but even while drawing the distinction, he makes it clear, in conformity with the process of rev-

47

elation, that he who sees the Son sees the Father; for the Son is the expression, the manifestation, of the Father without being the Father. The Son is the Word of the Father, so that He is God Speaking, God present; He is the Revealer, the Mediator; He is God dwelling among us (the ancient theme of the Emmanuel). Thus, despite the boldness of these formulas, St. John remains as monotheistic as St. Paul, and on this essential point, as faithful as he to the modes of thought of the Bible. Yet, because St. John uses a term that has multiple reverberations, he opens up new paths to Christology. Thus the theology of the Trinity was to be born from that of the Logos, and it was to discern in God relationships of consubstantiality between different Persons, the Father, the Son, and the Holy Spirit manifested at Pentecost.

6. Thus far we have seen how Christ was typified, in turn, as the Messiah-Prophet, the Messiah-Lord, the Messiah-Judge, the Messiah-Divine Savior, and the Messiah-Logos; He was given yet other names in other cultural environments. Truth to tell, the history of these new typological layers is very obscure, and the influences it reflects are quite complex. Most of the time, it is less a matter of the creation of new categories than of a phenomenon of interference in the transmission of old ones.

For example, the Greek terms *kyrios* and *soter* can each be read in two senses, which end by returning the same echo. In the Greek version of the Hebrew Bible, *kyrios* is used to translate *Adonai,* which replaces the tetragram of the Divine Name, the uttering of which still remained forbidden; the word *soter* recalls that God is salvation in the sense used in the Psalms (Pss. 7, 12, 18, 27, 98, 118, etc.). But *kyrios* and *soter* also evoke the imperial cults practised in the Hellenistic monarchies. Hence, in applying to Jesus these two titles, *Lord* and *Savior,* which had become traditional, we do two things at once: we designate biblical attributes and, at the same time, use titles of worship which were borrowed from paganism. This certainly rendered the spread of Christology easier, for hereby it was possible to speak to the Gentiles in a language they understood without departing from the sound basis of the vocabulary of Scripture.

In the same way, the myths and rituals of the mystery religions (of the gods Osiris, Attis, Adonis, Mithra) made the story of the crucified and risen Lord more acceptable in the East and West. Some critics have even thought that these cults influenced the story of the Passion and Resurrection of Christ, or at least that they influenced the interpretation that St. Paul gave to those events. But no one has offered any proof of this view; and, moreover, the differences between the cults and the theology of St. Paul are so marked that the few similarities are not convincing. Nevertheless, because of the general atmosphere of these cults and their modes of expression, it is possible that they did help in the understanding of redemption by Christ. At any rate, they did much to support the belief in immortality. In this connection, they shared the idea of a glorifying divinization, of a grace that brings immortality. Without this contribution, Christology perhaps would not have taken on certain emotional qualities which made it more suitable to the conversion of pagans. To be won over to Christ was to meet the Liberator, Him who removed the yoke of blind fate; it was to put one's trust in the brotherly giant who raises his friends up from the morass of earth and bears them to glory.

7. Although charged with many different meanings and rich in mystical values, the Messianic *type* achieved its final high place only by way of a philosophical advance—by approaching the subject as a metaphysical problem in order to arrive at a dogmatic definition.

At first glance, the definition has little resemblance, in its technical language, to the initial intuition, yet it is the flowering and crowning of that intuition. The Council of Chalcedon (A.D. 451) and the Second Council of Constantinople (A.D. 553) decreed that Christ is God and man, true God and true man, or better, that He is the God-man. By avoiding the affirmation that Jesus is God *simpliciter,* the faith counters the danger of pantheism (man is God) and eliminates Docetism (the humanity of Christ is a mere appearance). By not contending that He is man *simpliciter,* the faith confirms that Jesus is the Revealer of God, that He is God manifested and incarnate: this means that divine revelation really exists only if the Revealed is present in His Revealer, and only if Revealed and Revealer are at once one, and two, in the act of revelation. Now, this is a line of reasoning which is very much in agreement with the process of biblical revelation, as we have seen in regard to St. Paul and St. John. For there has been no severance from the biblical source, but only an elaboration of the original idea with the help of a more learned method and a more exact terminology.

When dealing with the man Jesus, it is easy to distinguish between the Revealed and the Revealer in their union, for the pertinent historical passages serve as a point of reference and show Jesus as the Son of God over against God the Father. But the distinction is more difficult to establish on a transcendental plane, between the Eternal Word and the formless Absolute evoked in Exodus 3:14. Almost four centuries of theological debate were needed to resolve this problem, a debate that subsequently led to the perfecting of the dogma of the Incarnation. The Christian faith then, at long last, arrived at a formula of reconciliation.

In order to safeguard the three terms mentioned in the New Testament—Father, Son, and Holy Spirit—the Christian faith has called them *Persons,* a concept which is itself polyvalent but which has the advantage here of marking the distinction between the three terms. In order to safeguard the oneness of the revealed God, Christianity has made Him a *substance,* again a multi-faceted concept, but in this context, the term strongly emphasizes the oneness of God's nature. Once the words had been defined, the two affirmations—the trinity of Persons and the identity of substance—had to be linked together. This task was performed by the councils of the fourth century, at Nicea in A.D. 325 and at Constantinople in A.D. 381.

The synthesis thus obtained would seem to be only a verbal solution. It limits itself to postulating simultaneously the *difference* between the terms and their *identity,* in accordance with the monotheistic imperative, without any consistently thinkable concept that would correspond to the result. But, as a matter of fact, the triadic structure as applied to the Gospel data contains an inner dialectic whose rationality can be respected. To hold that God is one and yet that He is neither monadic nor dyadic, but *triadic,* is to discover the important truth that the Absolute can be neither subject only, nor object only, nor even subject-object. The Absolute cannot be a solitary subject because every subject presupposes an object; nor can He be an isolated object, because every object presupposes a subject; nor can He be a subject-object because there is an incomparability of the terms, a falling away from each other which contradicts the idea of infinite energy. These difficulties can be resolved only by postulating the coexistence of three distinct subjects in the unity of one and the same object.

The Greek and Latin Fathers often professed belief both in Unity and Trinity, while only suspecting the implications of their view; but several theologians in the Middle Ages brought them plainly to light, with the result that they were accused of introducing a "rational" necessity into the being of the Trinity. Their argument was more or less as follows.

God is not alone, but expresses Himself in the Word; nor is He twofold, because the Son, the Word of the Father, must be as active as He in order to remain totally expressive. Hence the Father and the Son conjointly produce a third term. The third is co-equal with the Father and Son, as He must be if the divine energy is to be sustained at the same level of efficacy; moreover, He is distinguished from them in order that they may be distinguished from each other. The Triad is, therefore, not accidental but necessary; or it is so, at least, if one maintains that the Absolute integrates and surpasses the subject-object relationship which, in the human order, defines all thought. And theology does maintain it, for this position follows from the contention that Revealer-Revealed are at once identical and non-identical.

It will be observed that even if the divine "processions" can be rigorously deduced from certain premises, the mystery of God is none the less complete. The fact is that this mystery is beyond all rational dialectic. The Absolute transcends the categories of subject and object, but as reflected in them, it is triadic—a paradoxical conclusion that is reached, still more paradoxically, by meditation on the Gospels. But in order to preserve the infinity of the Absolute, we must go beyond our secular categories (subject-object) and even our religious categories, because the triplicity stressed by the New Testament, and which is obvious there, must be balanced by a unity that is not obvious. The mystical theologians who speak of God as *Super-Unity* and *Super–Trinity* show the path to follow. The dogma of the Trinity can have only one meaning for Christianity—a requirement that unity and trinity be corrected one by the other, in order to move in the direction of what is beyond all determination. Monotheism thus remains intact; and, at the same time, the "revealed" data fulfill their role exactly, which is to evoke and lead into a religious intention.

Must the "type" of the Messiah draw us into these subtle speculations? There is no doubt of it, because it was the position to be assigned to the Revealer which occasioned the trinitarian controversies, a suggestive example of a wholly spontaneous idea that mobilized legions of learned doctors. Such fecundity in an idea will surprise those who think that the marriage of cultures is always a mere syncretism. Actually syncretisms are brilliant but ephemeral, whereas the continuous

growth of the typology of the Messiah in the environments of different cultures and its swift and durable results witness the fact that it drew strength from something
more than a chance-medley of elements. It increased and
it compelled recognition because it was rich in pos-
sibilities. Hellenism took it up from Judaism only because
it gave Hellenism, in its turn, an appreciable impetus.
Although it underwent a change of context several
times, yet it was never cut off from its roots; the proof
of this is that it pursued at every stage the "typification"
of the same historic Revealer, Christ. Such is the reason
for regarding Christology as being faithful to the typological canon of the Bible. The Christian faith applied itself to fashioning the "typical" existence and the
exemplary death of the theophanic subject, Jesus Christ;
and it urged its followers to conform their lives to that
exemplar, the vehicle of revelation. These two facts reflect the traditional lessons of Jewish typology. Hence
we have a heritage and the unending development of that
heritage. There is no break in the ways of its expression;
there is no discontinuity.

## Doctrine and Worship

Is this continuity strong in the practical order, too?
Do Judaism and Christianity view the relationship of the
particular to the universal in the same way? Again, yes—
and no.

Yes, in the sense that the principle is maintained
that the universal is necessarily expressible only through
the particular; also, that there can be an institution only
on these terms. Besides, Christianity, like Judaism, insists

that the religious community be the responsible con-
troller of everything it does as well as everything it writes.
From this point of view, they are both equally opposed
to the various forms of subjectivism and they demand
that private inspiration be referred to the common tradition, which is an indispensable condition for maintain-
ing unity in doctrine and worship. There is no doubt that
these rules have fostered the cause of universality, for
personal initiative can bear fruit in the social order only
if it acquires meaning and value for all, as it does for each.
In using a book as a witness, to which every believer is
referred, Judaism and Christianity succeed in institution-
alizing inspiration, fixing it and communicating it; but
here, too, fixation and communication presuppose communal agreement. Only tradition, in the collective sense,
judges the writings, ensures their being handed down,
watches over and guarantees their interpretation. That is
why the Church, like the Synagogue, set up a canon of
the Scriptures. She knew that there is no harmony
among subjects except through reference to a common
object. Moreover, history has impelled her in this direction with ever-increasing vigor, accentuating her hierarchical principle and centralizing her authority. Nevertheless, this historical evolution was not controlled ex-
clusively by the will-to-power of a few men. It came
about first of all as the response to an essential need:
because universality is viable on the institutional plane
only if it espouses the particularity of a group that is
firmly resolved to remain homogeneous in time and space.

On all of these points there is an analogy between
Judaism and Christianity, and that is why we have answered *yes* to the question. Yet we could as fittingly have

answered *no;* for, although the two movements agree that the universal is realized only in expressed particulars—Hegel drew his *concrete universal* from this idea—yet they differ in many ways. Christianity was Judaizing at the beginning, but it rapidly became a Judeo-Hellenism in the order of ideas. Furthermore, because of the influence of St. Paul, respect for the observances of the Law ceased being obligatory. The Christian sacramentary contains two rites inherited from Judaism, but a Judaism which we have called Essenian and which, as we have seen, was deeply affected by Greek and Iranian Influences.

The first of these two rites is Baptism, or the ceremony of incorporation into the Christian community, using water as a symbol of purification.

The second is the Eucharist, derived from the Jewish Passover meal and imbued with the mysticism of fraternal union which, among religious people, is associated with sitting down together to eat at the same table. In the beginning, it was called simply "the breaking of bread" (cf. Acts 2:42; 20:7), and it grew and rapidly became the center of the new worship. For St. Paul, and for Sts. Matthew, Mark, and Luke, the consuming of the bread and wine is the partaking of the Body and Blood of Christ. St. John, for his part, declares that Christ Himself is "the bread of life," that He is a manna far superior to that of the desert, and that the flesh and blood of the Son of Man are a spiritual food that obtains and sustains eternal life (John 6:54ff.).

In all of these authors, the two aspects of the Eucharist, the sacramental and the sacrificial are present and even inseparable, but in different proportions. Were St. Paul and St. John influenced by the ceremonies of the mystery-religions, in which the initiates partook of the cup of immortality? It is possible, but it has not been proved.

The Eucharist contains a double positive reference: first, to the farewell meal, which preceded the Passion, where Jesus blessed the bread and wine; second, to the sacrifice of Calvary, for the bread and the wine are separated as the Body and Blood of Christ were separated at the Crucifixion. Furthermore, the Eucharist draws its efficacy from soteriology as understood by St. John and St. Paul; that is to say, Jesus surrendered His body and poured out His blood to seal the New Covenant. In taking part in His sacrifice, the meaning of which was developed at the Last Supper on Holy Thursday and repeated in later celebrations of the Supper, which actively reproduce the attitude of making an offering, the Christian ratifies, on his own behalf, the New Covenant and receives its graces. From this point of view, receiving Communion is, in the words of St. Paul, "discerning the body of the Lord" (1 Cor. 11:29) and recognizing it as the principle of salvation.

The other Christian rites that theology regards as sacraments are of different degrees of antiquity. Confirmation and Holy Orders were adopted from apostolic acts; Extreme Unction is possibly of Jewish origin and is difficult to date; Matrimony unquestionably has an Old Testament foundation; and Penance later took on an auricular form, but reflects, through the *exomologesis* (public confession of sins) of the primitive Church, the penitential attitudes of the solemnities of Yom Kippur, the Day of Expiation. Thus, the Jewish derivation of the Christian ritual is amply demonstrated, but evolution has appreciably modified the primitive forms. The preponderant role allotted to the Eucharistic Supper, which was increasingly interpreted in the sacrificial sense and finally stylized in the Mass, has given Christian acts of worship an entirely new aspect. The destruction of the Temple in the year A.D. 70 contributed more than a little to encouraging the vigorous growth of this independent liturgy.

And what are we to think of the sacramental principle itself? Unquestionably it redounds to piety and fosters common life, for it consecrates communal activity without which the religious sense would be weaker and less sure. Certain critics are quick to denounce in all ritual the vestiges of ancient, primitive religion; they concede at best that the value of ritual is that of the myth it illustrates, no more and no less. This view is compatible with the concession that Christian ritual has a particularly high value and that, in fact, it embodies a salvation myth that one must recognize as noble and pure. But the fact remains that, in this view, Christian ritual scarcely rises above the level of benign superstition. In reality, the sacramental principle adopted by Christianity can be understood in two ways only: in the *magical* sense, if it involves an induced experience that ends in summoning up the presence of God; and in the religious and correct sense, if it means that the unity-in-difference of our human composite (and all of our ordinary behavior is *psycho-somatic)* rises to a pure spiritual recollection in God; and that we receive grace at the moment the outward ritual signifies it and thus confers it. It is the faithful who must choose between the two ways; it is the theologians who must educate them to choose properly: but only the second way avoids the danger of superstition.

Judaism and Christianity, besides differing from each other in their rituals, differ also in their ideas of salvation. Their conceptions of sin are basically the same, but in Christianity the moral element almost entirely absorbs the legal element. Moreover, the Christian faith, especially in the Catholic context, leads to a justification that is a personal renewal, the creation of a supernatural interior life, which is superior to any remission of the punishment for sin or any exterior kind of reconciliation. The Cross has eclipsed the burnt offering, and the Faith has overshadowed the Law. The Christian is not only absolved; he is reborn.

These changes in theory and practice are the result of a soteriology of a Christological kind, which is the essence of the great Christian innovation. The marvel is that Christology should have succeeded in assimilating so many disparate elements. Its plasticity has allowed the development of dogma and the evolution of worship, while it still bases itself on the historical Jesus. As a result of the Greek Fathers' philosophical thought, Christology has even been endowed with a metaphysical system admirably suited to defending its integrity. We can guess why learned men "took up" Christology: surely it was because of the theory of the Logos-Creator, which inevitably made the Word the matrix of ideas and reasoning. Thus, the progressive doctrinal development of Messianic typology gave rise to an *intellectualization* of the Christian fact, but not without controversy. Here we are in the presence of the only historical religion that was successful in systematizing the intuitive process of myth-making.

Here we see why the regret some people feel at seeing the Gospel encapsulated in dogmatic formulas is not necessarily a proper tribute to the freshness of the youthful apostolic faith. Rather, it may be a failure to recognize the principal merit of that faith, which consists in its ability to spread through all levels of consciousness, including the intellectual level. The dogmatic aspect of faith is not in itself a deviation but a breakthrough, for it is witness to the fact that the aims of Christianity stand up to the test when they are cast in speculative form and even in the form of rigorous logical deduction—provided, of course, certain presuppositions are admitted. Still, it is important to remember that a dogmatic definition is never a philosophical thesis, even when such a definition is couched in the language of philosophy. A dogma expresses a belief and hence it remains in the order of belief, not of knowledge. A dogmatic definition has the sole advantage of reflecting the religious *datum* in a culture and of laying the foundation for an understanding of the faith with the aid of rational middle terms.

The projection of the faith on all planes of consciousness is not without danger. There are the risks to which theological schools subject it through excessive intellectualism; then too there are the risks to which popular sentiment subjects it through a lack of intellectualism. We know that Christian typology has extended beyond Christology to the Blessed Virgin and the saints; but it is less well known that, in order to overcome paganism on its own ground, Christian typology, in its journeyings, has accumulated a number of peripheral beliefs and accidental practices. It would be less than honest to deny that the danger of superstition arises here once more. Yet this danger can be averted if the following particulars are kept in mind.

The calendar of the saints, which the Middle Ages did not supervise sufficiently, is only a secondary and dependent typology; Christ remains the sole archetype, the only Mediator, the one Revealer. In a word, He is the only source of things sacred.

Christian sentiment pays homage to the Mother of Jesus and to the saints, but only in relationship to Him and only in terms of the greater or lesser role that they play, either in sacred history or in the life of the community. The Blessed Virgin occupies a privileged place because of her motherhood, mystically enhanced by two attributes that exceed the limits of the human condition, namely, her exemption from Original Sin and the Virgin Birth, to which is added the complementary privilege of the Assumption. This threefold belief, which provides the structure of Mariology, seems a more fragile thing than Christology properly-so-called; but, in fact, this profusion of miracles, as the psychoanalyst C. G. Jung clearly saw, has altogether more strength and consistency than the fables to which some authors have tried to compare it. It is certainly impossible to accommodate in purely rational scientific discourse statements that belong to the sphere of mystical creation. But it is precisely within the mystical sphere that such statements are to be understood. A *mythologema* has meaning only in the context in which the mythical thought evolved. How much more, then, does sacred history, which is not simple legend but the controlled reading of certain events chosen from among thousands, have meaning only in the context in which its paradigms effectively operate. It would be a mistake to objectify the typical existence of the Blessed Virgin on the level of profane, and profaning, secularism. Religious authenticity is maintained by acknowledging in her typology the only power it claims to possess, that of further clarifying Christology, supporting its perspective of transcendence, and occasionally extending its eschatological meaning.

What we have just said about the Mother of Jesus applies also to the saints, but to a lesser degree. The saints too, as types, are landmarks of spiritual geography, besides being intercessors and protectors of the devotional psyche. Undoubtedly, Catholicism is greatly daring (and Protestantism condemns it) to allow the mediation of Christ to be diffracted, while the courage of Judaism consists rather in channeling its faith into one practice alone, the adoration of God. But what some call temerity is perhaps the result of calm assurance. When one has understood that Christ, as the Revealer, is the Alpha and Omega, one no longer hesitates to let the intervening letters fall into place. Moreover, Christianity is two thousand years old, which is not much time, yet a good deal. The surprising thing is not that it has been accused of focusing less than full attention on Christ, but that it is still as firmly centered on the Risen Christ as it was at the dawning of the Paschal faith.

It is possible that, to certain minds, owing to a lack of spiritual guidance or an excess of fear, this living center may lie somewhat hidden, with the result that the weight of the Christian faith is redistributed in accordance with factors that are not exactly those of the Gospel. Besides, it can be stated that in every religion it is the imaginative ideas that spread farthest and fastest, because emotion lays hold of them, and stresses and complicates them. It was no accident that the eschatology of life after death, as popularly conceived, was padded out with all the elements it encountered on its way. This eschatology could have been simplified by choosing to pursue one or the other of the two courses outlined in Judaism and Hellenism, namely, the resurrection of the body or personal immortality. Instead, popular eschatology combined them without synthesizing them: Jesus rose with a glorified body; St. Paul speaks about "a spiritual body"; the Blessed Virgin was brought up to Heaven body and soul; and the dead are without bodies as they wait for the general resurrection. But these representations, so little compatible with each other, are to be explained individually by different motives, sources, or contexts. The mistake would be to objectify them, to fix and harden them, as if one needed to assign a philosophical value to images that are, rather, aids to hope.

In the same way, the concepts of heaven and hell are daring projections into the next world, under a temporal and even spatial form, of the paired ethical terms good-evil, whose polar extremes are infinitely far apart. The merit of Christianity is not that it coupled these concepts so as to offer eternal happiness as a reward and suffering as a punishment, but rather that it transposed them and gave them a specifically religious meaning: heaven is the vision of God; hell is the privation of God, one or the other being freely willed by each person. This implies a certain conception of liberty, that of contingent choice, which is the easiest to teach when one is educating the masses. It is not necessary to dwell on this conception, because the aim of the Christian faith is not to impose a theory of freedom. First and foremost, the faith wants to affirm that only Christ saves and liberates. Eternal happiness then follows: it is present in germ here and now since grace is available to us; it will be given to us in its plenitude in the next life, when grace will produce all its effects. Sculptors, painters, poets, and preachers have created richly imaginative pictures of hell, because the very setting embodies retribution against oneself or against others. They have also depicted heaven, although more soberly, abstaining from the rather lurid realism of the Moslem paradises. They have "visualized" purgatory (expressing the need for purification) and have little difficulty describing the mode of existence of the "poor souls." When confronted with these representations, the theologian has always had the function of moderating them, of supplying the needed balance, and not of adding further color. In the end, we arrive at a consolidation of ideas, which marks the victory of good sense over popular sensationalism.

Similar remarks might be made about related notions. For example, demonology and angelology are accepted in Christianity because they play an incontestable role in the New Testament. At the time of Christ, the Sadducees regarded these concepts as modernistic notions, foreign imports, like the idea of resurrection, which in the opinion of many authors is of Iranian origin. Yet these ideas were accepted in many circles of Judaism. The angels helped many redactors of the Bible to preserve the transcendence of God, to spare Him from manifesting Himself except through envoys and agents entrusted with special missions. Later, when Judaism underwent Alexandrian influences, the angels achieved metaphysical dignity by becoming pure intelligences, an elevation that rendered them invulnerable to the theologians, while an iconography based on the Bible made them familiar to the simple faithful. Even the devils profited by a similar transformation. Broadly speaking, archaic tendencies in demonology, which were either fantastic (hostile animals) or animistic (disembodied spirits), gave way to ethical tendencies (the Devil as a fallen angel, as "Satan" or "the adversary" of the kingdom of God; the forces of darkness against those of light, etc.). In St. Paul the demoniacal forces are used to dramatize more effectively the human condition at grips with opposing powers. It may be observed that this type of explanation was especially helpful to him in overthrowing the gods of paganism, those of the astral-religions and of the mystery-religions. When religions are in competition, it is good tactics to borrow devils from the religion of one's neighbor. In the case of St. Paul, the tactic was justified because the pagan cults were effectively preventing the faith of Christ from spreading abroad. At any rate, this duality of opposed forces continued to be a necessity, in one form or another, in Gnostic systems of the Manichaean type, as well as in everyday lessons on the spiritual battle.

It is possible that, in certain connections—very few, it is true—Christianity bore the imprint of the Gnostic cosmologies and of the fantastic Judaism peculiar to the post-Exilic period. But it is pertinent to find out whether or not these were central representations or merely auxiliary ones. The apocalyptic orchestration of the Last Judgment does not in any way contradict the thesis of the actuality of salvation which one finds in St. Paul and St. John; so, too, the angelic or diabolical atmosphere of

Christian soteriology must not be allowed to destroy the essential truth that one is saved by love and by total dis-interestedness, as with Christ, while one is lost through pride and egoism, as with Adam. If this fundamental lesson wears a halo of darkness and confusion, it is because soteriology and eschatology are, by definition, of mixed composition, including as they do a correct, solid, irreducible idea to which clings a host of schemes and figments—all the dangerous and exciting things that popular imagination has been able to create. To affirm itself and spread through the Mediterranean world, Christianity had to move through Hellenistic syncretism; and it bears the marks of its journey. The important thing is to decide whether this disparity of background has obliterated its message or whether it has simply enriched its general symbolism. Furthermore, if one is to judge by the literary persistence of the Lucifer theme, one might conclude that man's fascination with the demoniacal is truly a constituent part of his awakening self-consciousness. In such a case, Christian demonology is not error but simply one dimension of spiritual experience, when we interpret this experience at a certain psychological level.

An eschatology of man and his world and an imaginatively wrought angelology and demonology made Christianity distinctive (and awkward to accept) even though it proclaimed its universality. But it must be understood that for it, as for Judaism, universality is not a promise of religion but rather a task, one which can be carried out only by the institution of the ideal, by an institution which, being historical and concrete, must also be limited and ambiguous. If we reduce Christianity to the commandment of love, everything seems easy, seems pure and unmixed; but the true state of affairs is not so simple as that. The precept of love is not a Christian invention. When Christ formulated it (see Matt. 22:37-39), He quoted two verses of the Jewish Bible (Lev. 19: 18 and Deut. 6:5). Thus it was from Judaism, and not from a different inspiration, that Christianity drew the great law of the Gospel: the love of God, who is not seen, finds its exact measure in the love of neighbor, who is seen—a statement fully in conformity with the Jewish spirit, which always makes the visible a witness to the invisible. But in order to spread this truth and to invite the people to live it, something more was needed than a password or a slogan, no matter how eloquent or generous. That is why Judaism and Christianity did not hesitate to institute the ideal, to institute love itself. This they accomplished by going back to the typological principle, which regulates internal attitudes, and to the sociological principle, which prescribes, organizes, and controls external conduct. If Christianity finally gained the advantage over Judaism, its source of inspiration, it is because Christianity evolved a fuller and more flexible typology, and also because it pushed to the extreme the formula of proselytism and turned resolutely towards the Gentiles, substituting a circumcision of the heart for circumcision of the flesh. Finally, and above all, it based its structures, both of doctrine and of worship, upon a historical Person, in whose presence no man can remain indifferent. But this threefold success could in no wise be explained without that starting point, which is incontestably to be found in the positive—that is, the historical and social—way in which Israel conceived religion.

# 4. Option and Institution

Following the exposition in the preceding chapters, it is perhaps permissible to propose the following definition: Christianity is the multiple and progressive *typification* of a historical Revealer; it is the worshipful, moral, and mystical imitation of its theophanic subject, Jesus Christ. Hereby it is both an *institution* and a *tradition,* that is to say, the established choice and handing down of objects, events, or persons which, in the Christian's eyes, manifest God.

Christianity can be defined in this way only because it has assimilated the three great structures of Judaism.

It is a *historical religion* because it regards history as revelatory and not nature, as do the pagan cults. On this account it is a humanism, because only man makes history and gives it a meaning. This discovery was the most precious and daring one made by the Jewish people.

It is a *typological religion* because it releases from the depths of history those personalities who are most suited to serve as archetypes, as exemplary guides. It makes of them privileged personages and stylizes them so that their attitudes may become model-attitudes, exemplars that call up the production and reproduction of behavior in conformity with the given ideal. And here, too, the Jewish people were the great instigators. Without their belief in the prophets and their Messianism, Jesus could not have become a type. And, indeed, He was typified in the Messianic style (He regarded himself as of the category of the Messiah), in the Lordly style (after the Resurrection), and in the Sapiential style—all these before He was typified (after the Fourth Gospel) in the Logomorphic style, as the Word, the theophanic incarnate individual.

Christianity is also a *universal religion* although its *expression* is a *particular* form of doctrine and worship. It preserves the goal of a transcendent Absolute within theoretical and practical structures, each of which has a date in history, bearing the mark of an epoch and the reflection of a cultural environment.

Such, it seems, is Christianity: at one and the same time a directed reading of history; a free and personal rediscovery of archetypal attitudes (meaning: the attitudes of those of our fellow men who contributed the most to making history); and finally, the deliberate adoption of traditional patterns, both in doctrine and in worship, as an index of transcendence and as institutional rules for religious life.

Phenomenology allows us to recover these various insights; we should be grateful to it for recalling that Christianity has meaning, that it is not merely an empirical collection of heteroclite ideas, and that, although it has moved through an enormous variety of cultural strata, it has succeeded in keeping stable and coherent its fundamental aim. However, phenomenology limits itself to describing phenomena and, in its own terms, does not permit the forming of judgments. Now, the philosopher does not merely want to witness the birth of a new meaning or the appearance of hitherto unknown values, even and especially when that meaning and those values claim to change the life of every man who comes into this world. Rather, he wants to know if this meaning is irreducible and if these values are authentic. The fact that history may be enthralling and the message it bears may be good tidings is of little use to him. He must ascertain whether they are true, and there, in the domain of critical truth, only the philosopher is qualified to decide.

Unfortunately, we cannot here propound in its full scope the question of the truth of Christianity, because our aim is phenomenological and not metaphysical or criteriological. However, in order to satisfy the reader's curiosity, I shall present some, necessarily limited, reflections which, in the absence of a systematic examination, will provide the suggestion of a judgment.

## Myth and History

First of all, by glancing back at chapter 2, let us confirm the fact that the principle of a historical religion, of a revelation that is immanent in history, is basically free of anthropomorphism. It would be a puerile interpretation of such a religion to see in it a contingent Absolute intervening at every turn in history to communicate its secrets and to make appeals for the restoration of order. This naive conception would seem to be warranted by the imagery of the Bible and by the ordinary modes of expression of a people who, though very intelligent, were for centuries not in the least intellectual. In fact and by right, the religious intuition of Israel far outstrips the language in which it is expressed. Although Judaism asserts that history is revelatory, this must not be taken to mean that the Eternal meddled arbitrarily and capriciously with the order that is proper to the human experience of history; and it must be understood that the Eternal God preserved this order so much the better in that He never suffered Himself to be immersed in its flux. The God of the Bible is ineffable, He whom no one has the right to name; He remains without face or form; He subsists beyond all determination; He is transcendent. That is why He never presents Himself openly. Human history alone serves Him as an organ of expression. "The heavens are telling the glory of God" (Ps. 19:1). Indeed they are, and this cry of the nomad who communed with himself as he gazed at the star-studded sky of the balmy Eastern night is particularly moving. But it is significant that it was man, and man alone, who succeeded in capturing and expressing this cosmic praise. Here is the great idea of Judaism: it is not nature that reveals God but humanity and the development of humanity, that is, history. When we say that history, in this sense, is revelatory, we are saying that revelation is an entirely human expression. Nevertheless, it remains of divine origin because the significance of human history is elaborated only from the human relationship with God.

Hence the anthropomorphisms of the Bible must not be imputed to God Himself, but rather to him who is speaking, who "is revealing," which is to say, man; they must on no account be attributed to Him who "reveals Himself" by and through man, which is to say, the Absolute. Moreover, certain critics have observed that the Bible accepts as divine attributes only anthropomorphisms of a historical or psycho-social order (e.g., God as king, God as father, and so on), and that it re-

71

jects all anthropomorphism of a purely natural kind (e.g., the sacred power as appertaining to a place, as shut up in a statue, and the like). This is a proof that man "reveals" God by his attitudes and actions insofar as they transcend nature, and not by the ends or products of his actions, mere objects in which his subjectivity subsists in an alienated state. Here one finds an authentic attempt to go beyond all naturalism and all determinism in order to set one's sights on God at the level of pure freedom; and it is this attempt that justifies and preserves the concept of "historical religion." At the same time, it gives us the measure of the genius of Israel. The Jewish people founded historical religion on that day when history became conscious of itself, in the minds of some few men, as the one prism capable of reflecting and revealing the Absolute, without distortion.

We have said that the Jewish initiative in relation to history was proof of its humanism, and there is nothing truer. In fact, it sees history as a deliberate orientation of nature, an assumption of responsibility for nature. Furthermore, it holds that the historical destiny of humanity stakes itself on an act of courage, which consists in a *bestowal of meaning*. This is a most valuable lesson for our times: Judaism is the antidote to the Absurd. For all will agree that the world, left to itself, is absurd; it has no meaning. But the Jewish people resolved to invent a meaning for it. Strictly speaking, there is no such thing as "the meaning of history" in the sense of a meaning fixed in advance: history has to be made. Israel chose to give it the meaning of a progressive consecration of creation, of a re-creation of the world, until the day when the world will express through peace and harmony the one ideal worthy of the name: the union

72

with God, upon whom man depends for self-realization and the fulfillment of all things. At the present time, no one should be ignorant of the fact that the will to orient history proceeds from the Hebrew tradition, regardless of whether we are speaking of the descendants of Israel or of the Christian or Islamic nations. We could add the Communist countries, even though Marxist intellectuals pretend to forget that their eschatology is a carbon copy of Jewish meliorism. For Hegel and Marx, this relationship would have nothing strained about it. Moreover, it is impossible to exalt history and incorporate into it, in one way or another, a messianic dynamism without rediscovering the inspiration of Judaism. And to assign as the goal of history, not the coming of the kingdom of God, but the disappearance of all internal contradiction, is not necessarily an advance. All things considered, Jewish eschatology was more realistic. It did, indeed, dream that the end of time would bring the triumph of man over the various forms of evil; but never, except for the shiftless and spineless, did it hope that a time would come within time when there would no longer be struggles or problems.

These observations are not sufficient to give a full account of the basic intention of historical religion in all its complexity, and still less to remove the disfavor into which it has fallen among philosophers, who are quick to discredit it as an archaic concept or a myth that belongs to the infancy of nations. Nevertheless, the idea of the unnamable God is radical, daring, and adult in conception. And the method that consists in having Him speak in and through history, in having Him say *I* as an absolute in dialogue and as an absolute in union, is witness to the fact, not that the Absolute is made in the image of man, but that man recognizes his capacity, by means of images and language, of aiming at something beyond all expression. Hence there is no fault to be found with the principle of historical religion. It can be called mythical if one wishes, because it speaks and because all speech is displaced from its object; but it is superior to myth and it even transcends the order of signs, to the extent that, through signs, it is able to reach the very thing the sign signifies.

## Typical Existence and Transcendence

The preceding paragraph enables us to grasp better the full purport of the typological method, which Christianity borrowed from Judaism. Even in religion, exemplarism remains extrinsic if the copy can be no more than exterior to the model. It is said of certain examples that they are more admirable than imitable, which means that these examples lack no virtue except being exemplary. But this is not the sense in which biblical typology should be interpreted. If the attitudes it regards as typical are reduced to simple pedagogical models, to mere outlines, there is a risk of never surmounting the exterior point of view; again, there are many cases called exemplary which it would be difficult and sometimes quite awkward to imitate to the letter. In reality, the typical is the revelatory (under various forms), much more than the imitable, in the ordinary and—to put it bluntly—the completely mechanical sense of that word. If Christ is to be imitated, it should not be done by any merely outward conformity, for this would lead to adopting His gestures, His manner of dress, and His day-to-day activities. Simple souls do not always know how to guard against servile imitation, but the schools of spirituality are more experienced and they speak about adhering, not to the external facts of the life of Christ, but to His inward states and spiritual dispositions; some of them even recommend uniting oneself to the interiority of the Eternal Word. And that is the heart of the matter, for to contemplate the typical existence of Christ is to seek to reproduce in oneself, not the external circumstances of that existence, but its essential inner elements. This comes down to perceiving a religious norm in order to apply it and to live it. It does not mean assuming a borrowed personality, as if one had to live the life of another in order to become oneself. On this point, the various programs of imitation, self-denial, and self-renewal can be misleading since they can give the impression that it is better to cease being oneself and to be absorbed into an ideal personality. Yet who would be so naive as to mistake completely the meaning of these appeals to self-renunciation? Losing oneself in order to find oneself has always meant only one thing, that the selfish ego must give way to the generous ego, which is the more interior and the only sound one. Happy is the man who, in carrying out this operation, has before his eyes the portrait of one who has accomplished it.

As we have said, the *typical* is the revelatory. In the Christian context, the designation is applied first of all to the supreme revealer, Jesus Christ. Now, His role goes far beyond teaching and leading by example, and therefore it must go much further than any mere prompting, no matter how effective. It must be understood that the specific function of the *type* is less to prescribe mimicry,

75

even if it is edifying, than to reveal or manifest a value. Religious exemplarism is hierophantic, for it witnesses to and incarnates the sacred. For the Christian, the life of Christ is theophany in action because it "shows" God or, better still, it actualizes the presence of God. Consequently, to imitate Christ is to unite oneself to the God of Christ, to unite oneself to God present and revealed in Christ. In this sense, the Christian has not only got to become another Christ, but he must *be* Christ, he must be united to God with the same love as Christ and in the same spirit. The great mystics understood this lesson, and for them Christological typology was no longer an opaque medium but was changed into a transparent mediation: it allowed the soul to attain God *directly* by a single totally effective mediation.

Now, this mediation must be properly understood, something that can be done only if the soul uses it correctly, that is to say, *intentionally,* for typology has no other efficacious way of working. Here too we have the exact meaning of typology, which has no reason for existence except hierophany itself: since God remains wrapped in His mystery man stands in need of objects that reveal Him. It is impossible to have the Absolute as one's goal and aim without expressing it in signs. It is for this reason that signs appeared and that religions are intentional symbolisms. We can enter into the proper perspective of these symbolisms only by taking their symbols as symbols, and by interpreting them realistically, since they embody an intention that extends beyond them, that extends as far as basic creative values, lacking which all religious expression would be pure non-sense. The intentional character of religious forms, considered logically or typologically, critically or spontaneously, is therefore the first thing that must be recognized. If one fails in this perception, superstition is not far off. The sign ceases to be expressive and becomes deceptive: it no longer directs the gaze toward the Absolute, which it signifies in a relative way, and it substitutes itself in place of the Absolute; that is to say, it becomes idolatry in the root sense of the word.

Is the intentional character of doctrine and worship, dogma and liturgy, always regarded? Is it, at any rate, properly regarded in this Christian religion in which the Man-God is Mediator? In this religion in which the Johannine Christ declares emphatically: "He who believes in me, believes not in me, but in him who sent me. And he who sees me sees him who sent me" (John 12:44 f.)? It is not for the philosopher to supply the answers to these questions, for his only right and duty is to declare that intentionality is the single path open toward transcendence.

## Mysticism and a Rule of Life: Five Presuppositions of Christianity

Of a particularized, institutionalized religion, does the philosopher have requirements that he can justifiably urge? Yes, because here also he is competent to mark the limits of what is reasonable. In principle, he accepts the fact that the universal presents itself as particularized, because abstract universality is outside psychology, outside history, and outside experience. For man, the intelligible is never given in its pure state, and consciousness grants it existence only in expressive signs. In linking the

77

universal with the particular, Judaism breaks no rules; on the contrary, it gives us meaning in its concrete totality and reminds us that the ideal and the experiential cannot be disassociated. Historical existence combines them in a thousand ways but never separates them; Judaism, by doing likewise, does not betray the regime of the incarnate spirit but rather consecrates it.

Once this principle, which is a condition for the possibility of all institution, is accepted, the philosopher asks to see how it is applied. He understands that three things are necessary for a religious institution: first, having intentionality of the Absolute, that is to say, a lived *mysticism;* second, an expressive symbolism, or a *myth* in the technical (not pejorative) sense; third, a rule of life, that is, an *organization* that renders the mystique viable by making the myth communicable. The philosopher can rightly pronounce the *dignus intrare* on every religious system that joins all three of these elements. Such is notably the case with Christianity. It has inherited from Judaism a mystical doctrine of transcendence that has nothing to fear from its rivals. It was born in the heart of a Hellenized Judaism whose cultural diversity, which is now better known, astonishes the experts. It grew up in a Graeco-Roman environment in which science, instead of destroying the faith, as it might have done, strengthened it by its teachings. Finally, it found in the West, not only theologians but also jurists, not only men of piety but also men of authority, with the result that it developed a precise code of laws and a strict discipline, both of which safeguarded its cohesion and fostered its expansion.

Having noted this, one should say that it is scarcely

within the province of the philosopher to judge in detail
whether or not the three elements enumerated above
always evolved in perfect harmony with one another. It is
possible to assume that the sociological element was
sometimes so overemphasized that it increased the am-
biguity inherent in every message, every doctrine; or
again, that the ideological element so hardened into a
system of concepts that it threatened to rigidify the
mystical life it was supposed to serve. In the same vein,
one might say that the legalistic Judaism to which
St. Paul was so opposed, and the Pharisaism condemned
by the Gospel, obliterated the prophetic inspiration in
whole or in part; and, in compensation, that Pauline
Christianity, following in the traces of Jesus, was a return to the true source and a revival of the true faith.
Then again one might speculate that the Christian re-
volution would have lost its savor with the passage of
generations, and that instituted religion would have become nothing more than an "established" religion in the
bad sense. But most will concede that the philosopher
need not respond to such questions, for only the religious
man, the man of faith, can, without impertinence,
measure the vitality of his faith against the religious
ideal that he professes.

Yet there is one point at which the philosopher
will freely intervene—a point that does not affect daily
religious practice, but rather the foundation of the
Christian institution. Is it possible, or desirable, or indispensable to *institute* human mysticism, to *institute*
grace, to *institute* universal love? Judaism and Christianity think that it is all of these, and it is just here
that they differ from all natural religions, all religions of

pure reason. Contrary to one accepted opinion, it is not probable that they invented grace and charity. Theories of the divinization of man, including the idea of "gratuitousness," can be found outside Judaism and Christianity in other mystical doctrines—even in certain philosophies, such as that of Plotinus—and the same holds good for the theories of love and reciprocity. On the other hand, Judaism and Christianity joined grace and the love of God, which is the source of love of neighbor, in well-defined schemes. It was peculiarly their idea that men discern the divine action in human situations. They signified that action in history, and they placed it at the heart of a given religious experience, that of the Jewish people and of the apostolic community. The Christian supernatural does not stem from the category of grace in general, which is found outside Christianity and which indeed asserts itself in every doctrine of transcendence. The Christian supernatural refers to a certain manner of instituting grace, that is to say, of making it manifest in a particular historical sequence and with the help of particular structures and rites. The element of positivity and concreteness is essential here, and to suppress it would be to suppress the faith itself. Under these conditions, institution does not appear as superadded but as constituent, and it is this that disturbs many philosophers. In fact they become reserved and hypersensitive the moment any meaning of a spiritual nature is linked, not to a structure (which is inevitable), but to a given structure to the exclusion of all others. Now, if a person is to call himself a Christian, he must hold that Christianity is valid because it is *the* true religion and not just one religion among others, or even the best of all religions. Christianity claims the privilege of being the only way of salvation; all other ways must be measured by it, to their resulting devaluation, even if they are conceded an element of truth. When the philosopher confronts this claim, he may be surprised and even shocked. Still, he does not have to abdicate his philosophic role, but should exercise his right of critical examination to the very end. Nevertheless, it is impossible for him either to use criteria external to the faith—they will not be valid since they are taken from outside it—or to borrow the criteria of the believer, because philosophical reason must see without the eyes of faith. In the last analysis, the philosopher has only one resource, and that is to point out, in all honesty, the basic options, the metaphysical choices, which the act of Christian faith presupposes. These options, it seems, are the following:

First, to admit that the Absolute exists and that it is not a fiction or a mere fancy. This Absolute is to be thought of as ineffable and undetermined, since it is transcendent; but one must believe that it *reveals* itself in history, where, as a result of the structures of history, it appears as an Absolute of dialogue, of union, and of grace that is prevenient, enabling, and so on.

Second, to consider that the sacred is a specific, irreducible value, as against those thinkers who assert that one's intentionality of God need not be expressed in the hierophantic mode and who explain that the quest of the Absolute can be pursued just as well in an ethical, esthetic, scientific, philosophical, and even philanthropical mode. This point of view must be denounced. It is essential to hold that the sacred is either an original

81

value, constituting a separate axiological order, and the highest; or else that it is a transcendental distinct from all others (although St. Thomas defines religion without appealing to the sacred) and not merely the religious dimension of the transcendentals. The fact that the unbeliever does not perceive this value is not an objection. Only he who lives by the sacred is able to bear witness to its existence, just as only the clearsighted person can attest to colors and the artist to beauty. However, the fact that certain people receive a quasi-mystical experience from other values does raise an objection. It must, nevertheless, be set aside: the sacred does not permit any profane value to be raised to the Absolute.

Third, to recognize that no communication from God and no participation in Him can exist without the sacral expression proper to any transmission of the sacred. There is no *hierogeny* without *hierophany,* just as in the philosophy of values, every *axiogeny* calls forth an *axiophany.* This is the classical position: there is no value without expression, no thought without words, no idea without an image.

Fourth, to hold that Jewish revelation, extended by Christological revelation, is the most appropriate sacral expression; that it outreaches and outclasses all others to such a degree that they are only approaches or inferior substitutes.

Fifth, to judge that each individual, at all times and in all places, from the moment that he accepts fully the Fourth point, just stated, has an unconditional obligation to join the institution that puts into practice on the social plane this expression of the sacred. Joining this institution involves accepting its teachings, putting them literally into practice, and, for the Roman Catholic, submission to the teaching authority of the Church.

These five points define the minimum conditions. In each case, they present a philosophical option in ascending order of difficulty. If a person accepts them, and only on condition that he does accept them, he has the right to think that Christianity is *the* form of salvation in our world.

# Appendix:
## The Philosophy of Religion and Its Past

Religion is more ancient than philosophy, as all agree, but few authors add that the philosophy of religion is as old as philosophy itself. Yet, that is the strict truth.

It is good form to say that philosophy began in the sixth century B.C. among the Ionians (Asia Minor), but it is fairly obvious that there is some arbitrariness in this assignment of origins. Is it likely that man began to ponder the problem of his destiny only when he started to inquire whether the world sprang from water, air, earth, or fire? In fact, man's concern about man is more ancient still than the verbal formulation of it, and it is a fortiori more ancient than the first formulations we have at our disposal. If Western history has such esteem for the Greeks of the sixth century B.C., it is because the Greeks of the following century preserved their predecessors' work, at least in part, and also because we have agreed to regard Plato and Aristotle as the best judges in the matter. We apply the term "pre-Socratics" to the Milesians, the Ephesians, and the Eleatics to emphasize that Socrates is the philosophical messiah who decides everything, to such an extent that we rearrange the past and orient the future in relationship to him. But this designation of Socrates as a reference point is necessarily a matter of choice, and "pre-Socratics" and "post-Socratics" are terms that express the realities of history only to the extent that we decree that Socrates is the center of the history of philosophy, that the Socratic method is the model for all philosophical method, that, in a word, the Greek way of philosophizing is the only way possible.

But things are not quite so simple. From Thales to Jean-Paul Sartre is less than three thousand years of the whole existence of man, which covers several hundred millennia. In other words, the history of our philosophy is very short. It is true that time has nothing to do with the matter and that quality is not a function of quantity. But has this quality manifested itself on so few occasions? Were the Greeks the only "chosen people" of the philosophical idea? Are we not being intolerably complacent in claiming that the West alone conceived, fostered, and perpetuated philosophical reflection? The sinologists and experts on Indian philosophy quite rightly denounce such sectarianism. Not only has the East produced "wisdoms" comparable to ours, but they did so before us. Likewise, the East succeeded in making these "wisdoms" flourish, not merely among an elite, but among whole segments of enormous communities, which was not the case with the Greeks. And their achievement was less by teaching in schools or other formal pedagogy than by more direct and concrete methods. As Paul Masson-Oursel has shown, the Oriental civilizations had a genius for making the masses think by using religious rites or acts (Judaism itself used this method). Besides, the exaggerated contrast between Eastern and Western thought is artificial, and the proof of it is now to be found on the historical level, seeing that the two cultures have exchanged ideas from the earliest times. They can be distinguished from each other but they cannot be made exclusive of each other, for they have come in contact at many junctures in the course of history.

Thus, to attribute to the Greek world alone the formation of philosophical ideas is nothing less than prejudice or ignorance. What is true is that the Greeks were the inventors of a certain formalism and that they perfected methods of reasoning which have never been equalled for introducing order into thought and continuity into action. Their logic may not, perhaps, encompass all logic, but it has an undeniable and effective rigor. Moreover, we certainly owe to Socrates the invention of philosophy as self-knowledge, or better still, as knowing the universal in oneself. Certainly, he did not secularize philosophy to the extent that is commonly held, but he did succeed in wrenching it from the confusion of Ionian polymathy. He gave knowledge of self pride of place over knowledge of the world, thereby really founding philosophy in the sense in which Western humanism understands it.

It would be a mistake, however, to believe that Socrates arrived at this point without the help of acquired knowledge. His initiative was not an absolute beginning but rather a crystallization, and it was dependent on the efforts made before him, although it may at times have reacted against such efforts. Now, even if it is impossible to go further back than the school of Miletus, it is clear that the thinkers of that school meditated especially on the cosmogonic myths of the religious traditions. Unfortunately, Aristotle and his disciples were interested in Thales, Anaximander, and

Anaximenes as physicists and meteorologists. That is why, even today, the Milesians are considered less as philosophers who rethought and clarified the ancient myths than as naturalists haltingly announcing the first rudiments of the sciences of geology and astronomy. In fact they represent the infancy of both science and philosophy, but in both spheres they used as their starting point the religious cosmologies that came to them from Mesopotamia or Egypt. From this point of view, religion is truly the mother of all thought, even among the Greeks, in that it furnished science a choice of images for establishing a first representation of the world. Religion also gave philosophy a sense of the infinite (Anaximander remembered this), of what is just and unjust, and what is perishable and imperishable (Anaximenes did not hesitate to divinize the primordial substance), thus going beyond the level of simple, positive observation.

Similar remarks must be made about the thinkers who followed. For Pythagoras and the Pythagorean school, religion and philosophy were in constant interaction. The School of Croton (ancient Italy, or *Magna Graecia,* ca. 530 B.C.) was much more a religious association modelled on the Orphic circles than a philosophical society in the modern sense, since its object was to form its votaries or initiates in the happy life. Yet, as against Orphism, its originality consisted of combining methods of purification, directed to immortality, with a mathematical symbolism whose aim was different from that of ritual and myth. It was a pre-philosophy of universal harmony; and although the discovery of irrational quantities restricted its ambition, it did not dry up its inspiration. Pythagoreanism was the great precedent that prevented Greek philosophy from becoming completely "laicized." It had far-reaching influence—it stemmed from the East and was well-received in the West—and as a result of this influence Hellenic thought preserved a religious dimension, even among the most positivistic of its philosophers.

Heraclitus, who lived in Ephesus towards the end of the sixth century B.C., was more scornful of popular beliefs, rejecting the Orphic mysteries and denouncing the practices of the cult of Dionysus, yet his cosmology remained as mythical as that of the Milesians. He declared his preference for what is seen over what is said, and he sought to make intuition prevail over tradition. The theories he developed were aimed at rationally determining the measure of the "mixed" actual world and at discovering the law, the *logos* of reality. Nevertheless, these theories were continuous with earlier representations of the world. The theory of contraries (the prototype of dialectics, whose driving force is internal conflict) is of the same order of intellectual maturity as the dualistic structures of Manichaeanism, and we know that the origin of the latter is lost in the abyss of time. Babylon, whose civilization flourished eighteen centuries before Christ, knew them but did not invent them. The idea of the basic unity of things, enduring despite incessant transformations and transmutations, moderated the idea of contraries and is said to be the less ancient, but no one can be sure: dualism and monism might well be complementary aspects, as they were already bound together in the mythologies developed by the men of archaic civilizations. At the very least, this idea of unity recalls the most ancient derivation of all things from a primordial element—the idea by which the Milesians placed so much store. The ideas of perpetual and universal flux, of contrasts that are at once unpredictable yet ruled by law, also recall the tonality of the primitive cosmogonies; it is through these cosmogonies, or in any case thanks to them, that these ideas present change as a becoming that is disconcerting yet fruitful, unpredictable yet harmonious. In a general way, it can be said that Heraclitus marked an advance over naive and spontaneous myth in that he stressed the law, the ordered measure of change; but one must add that his thought is sustained at the foundations precisely by the myths it claimed to surmount.

Parmenides (of Elea, sixth to fifth centuries B.C.) likewise combined two sources of inspiration, for he was a pupil of the Pythagoreans and also wrote in imitation of Orphic models. He opposed permanence and the identity of being to the becoming and change championed by Heraclitus, and for this reason he is the father of rationalism. But he knew how to reconcile a search for truth through mathematical method with an understanding of the sensible world through myth. Parmenides accepted both ways of knowing—a dialectic on the level of ideas, imagination on the level of opinions, beliefs, and affective needs—as Plato was to remember. Moreover, the union of idea and myth, this intimate collaboration between the concept and the image, seems to be at the core of philosophy. It is, in fact, the natural food of the life of the intellect, the rhythm of which is never made up of purely abstract reflections but is the mutuality and reciprocity of word and life, of sense and the senses.

It is unnecessary for our purpose here to dwell on

such pre-Socratic philosophers as Zeno, Empedocles, Anaxagoras, Leucippus, Democritus, and others. Some of these men were religious and others not; all were physicists and moralists in varying degrees. And all of them built upon the foundations laid by the Ionian thinkers. The original myths persisted to a greater or lesser extent in the thought of each. It even happened that these myths bore fruit in the very places where they were being fought down. Thus the Atomism of Democritus, in spite of its mechanistic, nonqualitative character, was still a myth, albeit a scientifically fertile one. Only the Sophists made much display of scepticism about the past generally, but it was only a pretense. The great Sophists took upon themselves the mission of saving art and culture, which meant that they did not reject a priori any heritage from the past. Their humanism was, above all, a guide for life in society, and they discovered that virtues of a political order exist, even if they were not able to formulate a true definition of them. This led them to neglect religion, which, Protagoras declared, was a subject too obscure for man, whose existence is so brief. They did not neglect morality, which they preached eagerly and often. They must not in any way be judged from their epigones, who ended in cynicism about society and in fatuous verbalism.

Socrates (470-399 B.C.), who wrote nothing and whom, like Christ, we know only through witnesses, is often regarded simply as a moralist. Yet he derived the precept "Know thyself" from a maxim inscribed on the façade of the temple at Delphi; his call to his special "apostolate" came as a result of an answer from the Pythoness (the priestess of the Delphic oracle). And also.

his personal "daimon" was a religious inspiration and not a profane intuition. The surprising thing is that this relationship to the divine was absorbed in a completely interior life, in a contemplation which he interrupted only to deliver his message of self-mastery. The religion of Socrates had no particular ideological or ritual content; or rather, unlike the Sophists, Socrates apparently respected the customary religion of his day, just as he complied with the laws of the city. He exercised his freedom of thought, and his freedom of speech (which was to cost him his life) when what was at issue was the definition of the ideas which were implied by everyday behavior. His calm irony then became the most imperative and the most purifying of criticisms. When confronted by Socrates, no one was able to define correctly temperance, courage, piety. Here was the proof that harmony with oneself, a consistency that is no longer notional but personal, is not to be achieved at the level of discourse; and it was the proof that self-knowledge fails on the objective plane and on the level of language that led to the admission that awareness of ignorance— "knowing that one knows nothing"—is the only virtue.

Must we see the Socratic method as a cultivation of scepticism in regard to reason and the concept? Of course not—at any rate, Plato thought the opposite. It should, instead, lead us to see that reason is mediation: the concept does not terminate in itself, but each idea leads to another idea, then to another, and so on endlessly. And we must also see that ideas taken in and of themselves are not sufficient, for they lead back to man, that is, to the knowing subject—the subject who, in knowing them, would be wrong to believe that he knows himself. The mystery of self, which is mystery itself, remains and is intact even after the test of dialectic. This is not to say that dialectic is fruitless, because only continual discussion and redefinition allow man to see that theoretical debate is endless, whereas practical reform cannot wait. It is curious that this lesson, which Plato learned and expanded, was sometimes neglected later, namely, the lesson that theory must be subordinated to practice, ideas to the Good, and essences to freedom. This is to proclaim the specific nature of the ethical and its primacy over the critical. Yet it is also to proclaim that the critical c l a r i f i e s and justifies that p r i m a c y and that only "learned" ignorance (*ignorantia docta*), only epicritical (and not procritical) practice is well grounded.

If we extended these remarks to the critique of religion, we would very usefully see that every philosopher of religion will profit from taking Socrates' attitude as a model, because, like Socrates, the philosopher of religion must admit that theory never completely exhausts practice, never replaces it, yet still plays an essential role therein. Thus, it is possible for critical reflection to bring its analyses to bear on whatever it wishes, since it follows its own laws and is master in its own house. But it must be careful not to reduce the mysterious, irreducible world of actions and conduct to its own system of ideas. Critical thought can be, and must be, the *word* of practical action; but it is not itself practical action. In this sense, the philosophy of religion is to religion what criticism is to practice. That is why religious values, which only the religious man can discern and appreciate in the order of everyday living, cannot be dissolved or explained away by a philosophic criticism, however radical and unrestricted. Obviously, these conclusions go beyond the findings of Socrates, as reported. What we know of him is quite general and imprecise, but it is certain that his example leads us to reflect in this direction: we must reason, argue, and define *in order to act*. And when we have spent much time in reasoning, arguing, and defining, we shall discover that harmony with self must still be achieved at the level of action, in the secret conduct of one's life. These conclusions have often been lost and found again in the course of the ages, and they could well be reconstituted without reference to Socrates; but we have just shown that he was their author, and it seems only just that we should recollect them under his name and place them under his aegis.

S o c r a t e s' most illustrious disciple, Plato (427-348 B.C.), adopted the attitude of his master and enriched it considerably. Although this short appendix is not the place to present an exposé of Platonism, it is important that we indicate the points at which Plato's philosophy is linked with religion: First, in its form, seeing that it repudiated neither mythical expression nor information derived from the experimental sciences; it thus recovered the sense of complexity and wholeness which characterized the ancient Ionians. Second, in its basis, seeing that Plato, like Socrates, spoke of divine inspiration, of daimonology; he held that all scientific knowledge should move toward contemplation of the Good; and he specified that the contemplative act must concentrate in itself all the powers of the soul. It is not always easy to connect the theory of Ideas, the dialectic of love, the cosmology, the ethics, and the politics contained in the *Dialogues*, because Plato's thought evolved and renewed itself at different stages of his life. At all events, no one can deny that submission to the unconditioned Good, to the Good "which is not a being," "which is beyond being," as well as the primacy of the practical, which Socrates had already stated, both witness an authentically mystical *élan*. Sometimes it is thought that this mystical element had little to do with logic or with epistemology, whose technical subtlety has, in comparison, the air of an intellectual exercise or of pedantry. But actually, in Plato, scientific knowledge and mysticism so interpenetrate that the destiny and immortality of the soul become a condition of the possibility of science. For the same reason, the component of myth, which might be taken for graceful diversion, rapidly becomes an original, if auxiliary, representation of the idea, and one which makes an indispensable contribution.

The Platonic myths are disconcerting for the modern reader, especially if he is a Christian, because they have neither the same basis nor structure as the typology to which the Bible has accustomed us. From the standpoint of literary quality, they are even too perfect for one to take them with the same methodological seriousness as the spontaneous myths of the old Hellenic cosmogonies. But they do not cease to be instructive. Apart from some passages of his *Timaeus,* Plato develops only anthropological myths, all of which are concerned with the history of the soul, its preexistence and future life. They embody the classical themes of genesis and eschatology, but they have the special characteristic that their images are often drawn from the scientific, geographical, and astronomical material which Plato had at his disposal. Genesis and eschatology are precisely what cannot be conceptualized, since there is no real experience of beginning and ending. Religions are much concerned with filling in these gaps in their rational scheme, for everyone wants to know what is essentially unknowable. Plato was fully aware of this state of affairs. Nevertheless, unlike modern rationalists, he did not balk at representing, at visualizing, matters that cannot be clear and distinct objects of thought. And why did Plato make this concession? It could be answered that it was out of condescension or some weakness. But that seems wrong. If, in fact, a myth is not a proof—and, in Plato, it usually comes into play after the proof—and even though, as Plotinus was to say later, a myth is only a projection in time of that which is outside of time, it is, nevertheless, the only form of thought that can penetrate consciousness at certain levels. Moreover, the myth is not a substitute for the idea, a kind of confused idea which would make do for a clear idea in vulgar minds. Plato did not make up myths so as to fly to the aid of those who had not understood the conceptual line of argument, but proposed them as a philosopher speaking to philosophers. In his eyes, the myth was not an understudy for the idea, nor was it its debased replica; it was rather the paradoxical radiation of the idea into the depths of consciousness, paradoxical because it illuminates indirectly: it regulates and proportions its light to the degree of receptivity of the lower levels of human consciousness.

For example, when Plato posits the preexistence of souls and extends them the power of choice before the fall, he does not intend to create time that precedes time, or an option that precedes effective freedom. He does not, therefore, betray the idea (if he had, his argument would have been self-contradictory); rather, he simply spreads it before the imagination and gears it to the movement of our sense and feeling. By doing so he safeguards the idea and succeeds in installing it in the very region where formal evidence could not establish conviction—in the depth of the psyche, the shadow-world, where the play of fantasy needs to be disciplined if the highest part of the soul is to dispose itself freely toward contemplation. From this point of view, myth is intended to "capture" the lower levels of the psyche so that the higher self may escape their counterattacks. This "capture" is undoubtedly captivation, incantation; and it may be that all myth operates at certain levels as a charm does. At least, this charm, this art of mastering the imagination, allows the idea to give free play to its self-affirmation without fear of a counter-offensive from the ordinary evidence of the senses and the illusions of the ego. And Plato achieved his ends: he does not lead us to believe that the soul preexists or that it predecides. He teaches, through the myth of forelife, foreknowledge, and forechoice, that our present life, knowledge, and choice are determined by ourselves alone. This is a valuable and effective lesson, which refutes the thesis of an anterior and exterior constraint on the exercise of consciousness. Joseph Moreau very properly writes: "Reminiscence (insofar as it is a myth) expresses the a priori character of knowledge in terms of becoming and historical succession. According to a method of exposition that was to be used in the *Timaeus,* reminiscence transforms an anteriority of principle, a transcendental relationship, into a chronological anteriority" (*La con-*

*struction de l'idéalisme platonicien* [Paris: Boivin 1939], p. 372).

What weakens the Platonic myths is that their author consciously elaborated them in the style of the fable; that is, he had the key to their meaning before composing them. But this objection is not altogether valid because the myths of genesis and eschatology, as well as the anthropological and cosmological ones, almost all stem from suggestions and sketches which predate the *Dialogues*. In fact, they are as old as culture itself. Having borrowed them from another tradition, Plato recast and reworked them; rarely did he create them in every detail. It can be said, therefore, that even in Plato the myths preserve the spontaneous, unitary character they had when they first appeared, a character that corresponds in man to his first apprehension of values. Plato did clarify and stylize the myths, but this is no bad thing: such simplification or finishing allows us to grasp better how he linked the mythic component to the essential idea, or more accurately, how the mythical prolongations of the idea, rightly form an integral part of the idea. As Joseph Moreau again says: "In this respect, it [the myth] is in no way allegorical; it is an intrinsic moment of scientific representation, just as indispensable to physics as diagrams are to geometry" *(La construction,* p. 419, n.1). In this perspective, incantatory explanation has different bearings: the image is not only subdued, but the orientation given it acquires the effectiveness of a structure, which from then on carries the idea, or which, rather, makes the idea "proceed" in the symbol, which causes the symbol to be inhabited by the idea.

In a word, Plato taught us with authority that philosophy must not be afraid to confront mythology, even to use, to integrate mythical structures. It is regrettable and strange that this lesson was later forgotten, and that so many historians of philosophy continue to treat the Platonic myths as something apart from Plato's philosophy, and sometimes even as a foreign body in it.

I shall merely make a notation of Aristotle (384-322 B.C.), for those of his works which have been preserved have very little to do with the object of our research. Aristotle had many interests: he was a logician, a physicist, a metaphysician, a naturalist, and a moralist. Thus his influence was felt in the most diverse fields when his books became known in the Middle Ages. Owing no doubt to his positivistic cast of mind, mystical inspiration properly-so-called occupied him to a very limited degree. Nevertheless, he affirmed the primacy of contemplation and developed a theology of the unmoved Mover, of Pure Act, which is "the thought of thought." This sober and parsimonious theodicy was taken up by St. Thomas Aquinas in the thirteenth century, but not without many modifications and additions. Aristotle's theodicy in its original form prepared the ground for setting the religious problem, but did not in fact set it. The Aristotelian God, with his immutability, was necessary for the equilibrium of the world, for its finality, for its hierarchical order; but knowledge of God and contact with God seem to have been denied to man. Hence it would be too much to expect to find in this context any detailed support for a philosophy of religion.

The Platonic tradition was revived by Plotinus (A.D. 205-207). Like the Epicureans, Plotinus broke free from the old tragic universe of religions and myth, and although he came under the influence of the Stoics, notably in cosmology and psychology, he was unwilling to accept the Stoic theology and piety. Nonetheless, he was undoubtedly the most religious of the ancient philosophers, a point about which the Christians, beginning with Pseudo-Dionysius the Areopagite, were not mistaken. Even today when Christian mysticism wishes to express itself, it spontaneously recites a lesson drawn from Plotinus' *Enneads* and handed down by Pseudo-Dionysius, Augustine, Eckhart, and John of the Cross.

Plotinus, however, dissociates mysticism from everything that is prayer or worship. He does not deny them a certain efficacy, but he fears the superstitious illusion connected with them. He seeks salvation only through the mediation of the intellect, and yet he demands that the intellect declare itself dependent and insists that attaining the intelligible is only a stage, although an indispensable one, on the journey toward the One, toward ecstasy. And since the One is transcendent, the final ecstasy presupposes a grace. As Jean Trouillard observes, only those who link "the idea of grace to that of contingency" can dispute the fact that Plotinus professed a mysticism of divine gratuitousness and liberality. Once the transscendence of the One is admitted, the plotinian ecstasy must be understood as a religious experience beyond the intelligible order. This amounts to understanding philosophy as an intermediary between two presences of the One to the spirit: the one a latent and unperceived presence, which constitutes the source of all spirituality; the other, a recognized and willed presence, which, in the dark night of language and meaning, of the senses and the understanding, consummates the marriage of intelligence with the Absolute. This is a unique case of an intellectualism that demands the mystical flight of the soul and conceives it as an access to untrammeled freedom. Spinoza, in the fifth book of the *Ethics,* was later to initiate a similar attempt, but he did not mark out so clearly the distinction to be made between intellectual effort and entrance into the supreme indetermination.

When we leave the Hellenistic period, we enter a Christianized world. From this point forward, culture embraces the relationship between philosophy and religion in a completely different way, as the relationship between reason and faith, between philosophy and theology. This new perspective is, broadly speaking, that of the whole Middle Ages as well as of modern times, despite the variety of positions adopted by different thinkers, whether or not they are believers. That is why we can be content with an overall view of the periods concerned. I had a set purpose in devoting so much time to the philosophers of ancient times. I did so because too seldom is it pointed out that Hellenic or Hellenistic thought always brought moral and religious preoccupations to bear on philosophical inquiry.

The Middle Ages could approach the religious problem only in relation to Christianity. Now, Christianity, which is derived from Judaism, is a historical and positive religion. There is not one instance of a Christian theologian and, until Hegel came along, not even one case of a philosopher, who tried to grasp the meaning of Christian positivity through purely rational reflection. Positive religion, as a consequence, was placed outside the field of philosophy and became the exclusive domain of the theologian, with the quite unforeseen result that there arose in philosophy a growing dislike for religious questions. Augustine, Erigena, and Bonaventure neither foresaw nor desired this rationalism, whereas St. Thomas accepted it with astounding audacity. He sorted out the truths of reason from the truths of faith, allotting the former to philosophy and the latter to theology. But, of course, he welded the two disciplines together: he distinguished between them in terms of their material and formal objects, but only to make them converge the more readily. However, in setting the philosopher to work on a separate order of truths, so-called "natural" truths in contrast to the supernatural truths reserved for the theologian, St. Thomas decided the fate of modern philosophy, which became less and less concerned about its complementary discipline, theology, and finally came to the point of seceding from it. St. Thomas was not responsible for this divorce; he himself retained the double competence of philosopher and theologian. Descartes himself was not responsible, for his dualism never went so far as to become a clean break, so much so that Malebranche was able to appeal to Descartes when rejecting this very dualism. Nevertheless, it cannot be denied that Thomism had a double effect in that it consecrated the autonomy of the philosopher, which was good; but it also, in all innocence, furnished the opportunity for certain minds to appropriate the title of philosopher without preserving any link with the professionals who were concerned with the religious problem. Now, this state of affairs is not necessarily beneficial, since dialogue with religion, pursued under different forms throughout antiquity and the Middle Ages, has never ceased to be a stimulant for the philosopher. So true is this that even the least orthodox thinkers have felt the need of renewing this dialogue—for example, Spinoza, Kant, Hegel, Comte, Renouvier, Brunschvicg, Alain, and others. Unhappily, however, they have tended more and more to approach religion externally, in a negative or polemical way, and have not often manifested a desire to understand religion in the sense in which the religious man practices it. Apart from Hegel, these thinkers have not been able to reintegrate into philosophy itself the problem of the positivity of Christianity, and that is their gravest lack.

It must be said in their defense, however, that they have had an excuse for what they did. Since the Middle Ages it has been understood that only the theologian has competence in matters of positive religion. It was only fitting, then, to leave him in charge. Spinoza, as an exegete and a former pupil of rabbis, drew up a critique of the Judeo-Christian Scriptures and was led obliquely to define the notions of revelation, prophecy, religious history, rite, institution, and so on. But in the end, instead of explaining them, he explained them away. According to his analysis, Christian positivity was neither comprehensive nor justified and was judged unworthy to be accorded philosophical status. He considered that he had good reasons for rejecting Christianity, and his exegesis was far in advance of his contemporaries'. Yet it would be unjust to consider his reservations as a condemnation pure and simple, although he did hold that religious positivity is not comparable to philosophical reflection either as a historical expression or as the determiner of doctrine or worship. This view is only one step away from alleging that Christian positivity has no meaning and that it has coherence solely for the theologian. This conclusion does not inordinately displease the theologian, because he, like all specialists, looks with a jaundiced eye on anyone who ventures into his territory.

But such venturing is necessary, and the philosopher must embark on it because he cannot accept the idea of forbidden ground. The province of reason is universal, or it does not exist at all—but on the clearly understood condition that the investigator must use a method adapted to his aim. In truth, the positive nature of religion is received by the theologian as a fact. He does not require of it that its truth be demonstrable on purely rational grounds. The Christian theologian takes Scripture and tradition as sources and objects of faith which immediately have the *value of revelation.* They serve to institute, promote, and regulate religious experience. They are not questioned, nor do they have to be. Theology starts with an act of faith; it initiates and develops an understanding of the faith, for which purpose it uses rational middle terms. These terms then react on the principles of faith and permit rational conclusions to be drawn from them, but with continued adherence to the faith-value of these principles. In a word, the theologian uses his reason to understand his faith, but always in dependence upon and in the light of that faith. Thus it remains for a properly philosophical reflection to be applied to the religious datum, something that is in no way a threat to the development of theology. A strictly rational critique must still be made of the religious fact, but without denying a priori that Scripture and tradition may have a revelatory significance for the believer. As a result the whole of religious positivity is thrown open to the philosopher, so that he may examine it to its foundations from a point of view that does not imply in itself an act of faith. This is a daring and delicate, but indispensable, step to take. If it is not attempted, religious experience will continue to be viewed with suspicion; the philosopher will retain the impression that he is not trusted and he, in turn, will become distrustful.

Hegel deserves to be regarded as the first philosopher of Christian positivity, the first philosopher, that is, of religious institution. Kant, by reason of his moralism, did not understand the specific character of mysticism in relation to ethics, nor did he admit the link between faith and historical structures. Schelling gave an interpretation of myth and revelation which is often very rewarding; but he declared that the positive or instituted element is always secondary in religion; the primary religious form is essentially natural, its expression being mythological (in the pagan sense) and not intentional and volitional. Now this seems debatable, for it is to suppose that man could live humanly before he was the institutor of meaning. Hegel avoided this mistake. For him positivity, at least good positivity (for there is a bad. positivity, which never has any possibility of *knowing* its own meaning), is a necessary moment in dialectic. Every spiritual experience and every human advance, if it is to be coherent and complete, should lead to expression, to concrete realization, to mutual communication. This detour through exteriority is obviously not the end of the process; one must return from outside in, just as one first had to pass from inside out. Reintegration closes the circle and does so effectively by the fact that the experiential, having expressed the ideal, knows the possessing of it in and by expressing it. This conception retains something of the abstract and the artificial in the way it is stated; but reduced to this essential scheme, relieved of all excess baggage, it surely lays the foundations of positivity and, in fact, gives it an expressive value that is not accidental but necessary. Instated in this context, historical religion of the revealed type is no longer a fact that is unassimilable by the philosopher, but is, by virtue of the law of expression, an authentic figure of the Absolute. That is how Hegel understood it. There would be nothing to add to his interpretation if, first, he had not held that the historical process involves the Absolute as the direct subject of history, whereas history is really the record of man's reaction to a transcendent Absolute; and, second, if he did not teach that religion achieves meaning only through the efforts of the philosopher, whom he considers to be the only faithful interpreter of the dialectical movement. These drawbacks prevent us from being content with Hegel's philosophy of religion, but it would be vain to attempt an understanding of religious positivity without having at least "encountered" this philosophy.

It is only in the contemporary period, in the wake of Husserl's phenomenology, that we find an elaboration of the philosophical understanding of religion which pursues an end other than that of condemning or bypassing religion. Husserl himself did not apply his method to religion, but some of his disciples did it for him; for example, Scheler, who was not much concerned with positivity, and G. van der Leeuw, who was constantly preoccupied with the problem of reinstating the religious phenomenon in the context of history. Van der Leeuw's method, which was also pursued by Maurice Blondel, consists of describing positive religion as it presents itself, and setting forth the precise meaning it claims for itself, but prescinding from the life values discovered in it by the believer. Religious structures such as rites and dogmas are examined one by one and are analyzed with no other aim than to sustain the meaning of each part in relation to the whole. If that were not done, the religious phenomenon would be treated, not as religious, but as moral, social, political, economic, literary, aesthetic, and so on. The present book employs this kind of method. Its advantage is that it enables us to understand, without having to accept or reject, the ontological validity of the ideas under discussion. Religious phenomenology thus proves worthy of respect, owing, it is true, to a suspension of judgment.

Many authors go no further: they describe but do not come to any decision. Yet judgment remains by right the function of the philosopher; accordingly, if religious phenomenology is to become a philosophy of religion, then judgment must be added to description. Personally, I believe that this is possible, desirable, and even necessary, but on the one condition, that the philosophical critique hold rigorously to its own role. It is good that it should take the initiative of discussing and evaluating everything; but it ought also to become aware of its own presuppositions and postulates. It must verify that its conclusions and its premises are in logical agreement. Finally, it must recognize the specific nature of practice, and the fact that practice cannot be reduced to theory or critique. It has to determine the conditions for the possibility and validity of the religious act, but it must not reduce the act itself to these conditions, nor must it absorb or dissolve the act in the theoretical elucidation of these conditions. Learned morality is not lived morality, although the one does elucidate the other; likewise, although the philosophy of religion is not effective religion, it does clarify the meaning of effective religion and define the limits of its kind of efficacy. This may be a useful reminder to those who are tempted to confuse *knowing* and *doing.*

The only harm that could be done to the faith by this philosophic method would be if it proved that religious values were illusory and deluding. But who is going to prove so much? The unbeliever does not hold these values and cannot judge them. The believer lives them as something original and distinct from all other kinds of values. But he lives them without being able to objectify them. By objectifying them, he would, by the very fact, destroy them and deprive himself both of the joy of living them and of being able to bear testimony to them. The truth is that, although one can criticize the expression of a lived experience, and hence its declared object, such a lived experience can be apprehended in itself only by experiencing it. This is so because existence is not proved but rather experienced. If one does not experience it, one can only be silent—moaning and cursing are useless. Any other attitude would be like allowing a blind man to deny that colors exist, or a philistine to belittle art, or a fool to declaim about the wise man's "folly." This would lead to an absurd, if picturesque, world. But who would want to identify such a world with the world of philosophy? Instead, let us give philosophic criticism a role that is comprehensive enough to ensure that everything "criticizable"—everything that can be analyzed, and evaluated—is made to pass its scrutiny. If there is anything inconsistent or incoherent in religion, criticism will discern it. Now, religion cannot exist without being reflected in words or manifesting itself in a mode of conduct. Hence, if religion itself is only a parasitic activity, the result of fear or oppression, criticism will be able to discover the fact and utter it.

At any rate, no one will deny that our era is one in which philosophical discourse has once more learned how to nourish itself on ideas that through the ages have waited in vain for reason to develop them. Judaism invented the categories of history, revelation, faith, sin, and others. Judeo-Christianity gave pride of place to the categories of incarnation, person, witness, charity or pure love, and others. Now, the *philosophical* elaboration of these categories had scarcely begun before the nineteenth century, and even so, several of them were not rehabilitated by the philosophers until about thirty years ago. At that time some historians and scholars asserted that by adopting these categories we were returning to the pre-Socratics; some rationalists protested that myth or religion, under the influence of Kierkegaard, the existentialists, and the phenomenologists, was reappearing in the temple of reason, perhaps in borrowed clothing— and they were not completely wrong. But it is important to persuade them that the natural climate for philosophy is not the thin air of the study, but rather the atmosphere of life, and life in all its forms—scientific, moral, aesthetic, and religious. The system of ideas, which certain thinkers naively confuse with the chains of argument which they keep locked up in their books, is not mere academic logic. Instead, it is one with the huge effort of history and culture, and no man can isolate it or wall it off or say that it begins here and ends there. To perceive its meaning, one must hear not only the melody of one or the other particular discipline but the symphony of the whole cultural universe. There is no idea that stands independent and apart from the background of myths and religions. The most abstruse concept still has its roots in imagery, which remains the only witness of its belonging to the human complex. We should rejoice that the need for total integration is so strongly felt in contemporary philosophy, even if, for the time being, it causes quite a lot of confusion. These riches should not embarrass us. Things will eventually get sorted out and reclassified. It is better to have an anthropology as wide as the world than a bare algebra of notions or a mere residue of abstractions. I say this, not because I prefer agitation to lucidity, but as a reminder that reflective thought ought to be coextensive with human experience and should resolve to become so in fact.

It is possible that this wish to welcome life and to bring all of it together—and without constructing obscurely on its margins, may forever wither the inspiration that has built up the great metaphysical systems. But who would regret it? The purely critical function of philosophy must be returned to it without remorse and without useless nostalgia. The philosopher always arrives *after the event,* after existence, after history, after the fact, and he can recapture only what is already there, the meaning already uttered and already instituted. Whether we like it or not, our only hope for the future of philosophy is to be henceforth both *culturalists* and *institu-tionalists.* The time is past when culture could be regard-ed as the extension or the almost unchanged transposition of nature, an attitude that was an illusion even on the first day of what we know as civilization. Man knows nature only in humanizing it, and he knows only a nature already humanized. Even the members of primitive societies could not dissociate the *natural* from the *cultural,* and they simply rearranged time and space ac-cording to their convenience. Let us, then, take up our position in front of the fact of language, the fact of the great collective myths, the fact of the arts and sciences and religions, for the task of the philosopher is to study, analyze, and judge them. It is his function to take ac-count, not of ideas alone, but also of institutions, under-standing this term in its widest sense. Religion is one in-stitution among others, and there is no reason why the philosopher should examine all institutions except this one alone. Resentment against religion or false respect for it has nothing to do with a reflective attitude. By return-ing to religion without bias, sympathetically yet indepen-dently, the philosopher will give to some an example of objectivity, to others an example of intellectual cour-age, and to all a lesson in composure.

# Bibliography

*Source*

*La Bible, Ancien et Nouveau Testaments,* Editions
Crampon-Bonsirven-Tricot; L. Segond. See also the
Jerusalem Bible (Cerf), the Lille edition (Letouzey),
and the Maredsous edition (Zech).
*The Holy Bible.* Revised Standard Version, Catholic
Edition. London: Catholic Truth Society, 1966.

*Studies*

Baron, S. W. *A Social and Religious History of the Jews.*
14 vols. New York: Columbia University Press, 1952-
1969.
Bonnes, J. P. *David et les psaumes.* Paris: Le Seuil, 1957.
Bonsirven, J. *Le règne de Dieu.* Paris: Aubier, 1957.
Bouillard, H. *Karl Barth.* Paris: Aubier, 1957.
Bouyer, L. *La Bible et l'Évangile.* Paris: Le Cerf, 1951.
Buber, M. *Moses: The Revelation and the Covenant.* New
York: Harper and Row, n.d.
Bultmann, R. *L'interprétation du Nouveau Testament.*
Paris: Aubier, 1955.
Cerfaux, L. *La communauté apostolique.* Paris: Le Cerf,
1953.
Chenu, M. D. *La théologie, est-elle une science?* Paris:
Fayard, 1957.
Cullmann, O. *Christ and Time.* Rev. ed. Philadelphia:
Westminster, 1964.

Cuttat, J. A. *La rencontre des religions.* Paris: Aubier, 1957.

Daniélou, J. *Sacramentum futuri. Études sur les origines de la typologie biblique.* Paris: Beauchesne, 1950.

———. *Les manuscrits de la mer Morte et les origines du christianisme.* Paris: L'Orante, 1957.

Davis, G. W. *Existentialism and Theology.* New York: Philosophical Library, 1957.

Dibelius, M. *Botschaft und Geschichte.* 2 vols. Tübingen: Mohr, 1953-1956.

Draguet, R. *Histoire du dogme catholique.* Paris: Albin Michel, 1941.

Duméry, H. *The Problem of God in the Philosophy of Religion.* Translated by C. Courtney. Northwestern University Press, 1964.

———. *Critique et religion.* Paris: Societe d'Édition d 'Enseignment supérieur, 1957.

———. *Philosophie de la religion.* 2 vols. Paris: Presses Universitaires de France, 1957.

———. *La foi n'est pas un cri.* Paris: Casterman, 1957.

Eliade, M. *Myths, Dreams and Mysteries.* New York: Harper and Row.

Giet, S. *L'Apocalypse et l'histoire.* Paris: Presses Universitaires de France, 1957.

Griaule, M. *Méthode de l'ethnographie.* Paris: Le Cerf, 1952.

Guérard des Lauriers, M. L. *Dimensions de la foi.* 2 vols. Paris: Le Cerf, 1952.

Guitton, J. *Jesus.* New York: Alba House, 1968.

Gusdorf, G. *La parole.* Paris: Presses Universitaires de France, 1953.

——. *Mythe et métaphysique.* Paris: Flammarion, 1953.

——. *Traité de métaphysique.* Paris: Colin, 1956.

Kimpel, B. F. *Language and Religion.* New York: Philosophical Library, 1957.

Lacroix, J. *Les sentiments et la vie morale.* Paris: Presses Universitaires de France, 1952.

Le Roy, G. *Pascal savant et croyant.* Paris: Presses Universitaires de France, 1952.

de Lubac, H. *Sur les chemins de Dieu.* Paris: Aubier, 1956.

Mehl, R. *The Condition of the Catholic Philosopher.* Greenwood, S.C.: Attic Press, 1963.

Nédoncelle, M. *Existe-t-il une philosophie chrétienne?* Paris: Fayard, 1956.

——. *Vers une philosophie de l'amour.* Paris: Aubier, 1957.

Neher, A. *Prophetic Existence.* New York: Barnes, 1969.

——. *Moïse et la vocation juive.* Paris: Le Seuil, 1956.

Pepin, J. *Mythe et allégorie.* Paris: Aubier, 1958.

Ricoeur, P. *History and Truth.* Evanston, Ill.: Northwestern University Press, 1965.

Rowley, H. H. *The Faith of Israel.* London: S. C. M. Press, 1956.

Schmidt, A. M. *Jean Calvin et la tradition calvinienne.* Paris: Le Seuil, 1957.

Simon, M. *Les premiers chrétiens.* Paris: Presses Universitaires de France, 1952.

Steinmann, J. *La critique devant la Bible.* Paris: Fayard, 1956.

Teilhard de Chardin, P. *The Divine Milieu.* New York: Harper and Row, 1960.

113

Tresmontant, C. *Christian Metaphysics.* New York: Sheed and Ward, 1965.

Vancourt, R. *La phénoménologie et la foi.* Paris: Desclée, 1954.

——. *Pensée moderne et philosophie chrétienne.* Paris: Fayard, 1957.

Van der Leeuw, G. *Religion in Essence and Manifestation.* New York: Harper and Row, n.d.

Wahl, J. *Philosophies of Existence.* New York: Schocken, 1969.